BRAMPTON BOY

BRAMPTON BOY

A SOLDIER'S BATTLE
OF LIFE AND FAITH
IN THE FIRST WORLD WAR

David Christopher Middleton

First published in Great Britain in 2018 by

Bannister Publications Ltd
118 Saltergate
Chesterfield
Derbyshire S40 1NG

ISBN 978-1-909813-47-2

David Christopher Middleton asserts the moral right to be identified
as the author of this work

A catalogue record for this book is available from the British Library

Typeset by Escritor Design, Bournemouth

Printed and bound in Great Britain

To my beautiful wife Jayne who, on many holidays sat patiently reading, whilst I scribbled on napkins and scrap paper.

Contents

Introduction

As with lots of things in life, you put them to the back of your mind and think: "I will do that one day". It was only after the coverage of the ninety years since the Great War, and the stoic stories of *The Last Tommy* by Harry Patch, that I felt inspired to find out a little more about the part my own Grandfather Chris had played in the First World War. As a small child I have very fond memories of the nicest grandfather in the world. I can still see him now in his open-necked shirt, bib and brace overalls, and a cigarette in the corner of his mouth, pushing me in his wheelbarrow back from his allotment accompanied by the sound of his hobnail boots.

When he died I was given a small Bible as a keepsake in which, inside the front cover, his army details were recorded, together with a very poignant message from his father, my great-grandfather. Having Internet access to all service records, I used this information to track down his war service records. I was very lucky because in the Second World War a direct hit by an incendiary on Grosvenor House meant that many WW1 records were lost completely, or in my case as you can see, burnt around the edges but still legible. Together with Joan his daughter (my mum) and with her suitcase of memorabilia, I managed to piece together interesting photos and details about his life.

It was only when I had finally compiled it all and was reading through it with my mum that she broke down and told me of something that wasn't to be found in any official records; something very controversial that had left Christopher traumatised all his life and may leave you, as a reader, in two minds about Chris the person. But his story needed to be told as I don't think it was unique.

I have therefore tried to bring Christopher, a local Brampton lad, back to life for you. It starts with him working his final days at the gas board, and then as a small boy growing up in Brampton during these tumultuous violent times. Hopefully, you will be able to experience living with him and his unbelievable stories of his war years, and appreciate what it was like to be caught up in WW1, and his later involvement in WW2. I hope you can see what sort of character he was

1

and the life he had. It is all based and interwoven with his actual army records and factual stories that were researched by my brother, Brian.

This was many years ago before the Internet and when my family members were still alive, and he was able to ask questions of all involved. Then there are all the stories and conversations I heard our family talk about as I grew up. I have tried to consolidate all these memories of this very special man and put them down on paper, interweaving them with my mother's own very detailed stories of her early childhood and her parents' life.

Sadly she was diagnosed with early onset dementia during the time I was trying to get many of her accounts written down, but amazingly, she was able to remember events from 60–70 years ago in such detail and with such clarity, despite not being able to recall what she had just had for lunch. I have also tried to include local history, which as I now get older myself is also important to record, and so I will be donating a copy of this book to Chesterfield Library and the National War Museum.

David Middleton
Chesterfield, 2018

Chapter 1

Another Day...another Trench

He was back there, and it seemed all so real. Was it just his donkey jacket that weighed heavy with filth and in the drizzle or his boots welded to the floor in the thick sludge that reminded him? There was a strong smell of gas seeping from the main he had cut into, sealed with a cricket ball-sized lump of clay as a temporary bung, and then the noise: that stomach-vibrating noise. A concerto emerged from the petrol road compactor jumping up and down with its distinctive *err thrump clatter*. It was backed by the droning of the diesel compressor racing and slowing with a whoosh of escaping air, just like a passing shell. All this was serenaded with the *rat-tat-tat* from the jackhammers cutting through the tarmac into the soft clay. He felt his stomach tighten, his hands shake, and cold sweat break on his brow. It was going to be one of his bad days. Chris hauled himself up the ladder. He could see people going about their business further down the street. He threw a large adjustable wrench onto the spoil at the side of the trench. It landed, making a sound just like a bolt on a rifle, and in his mind he had already fired off two shots, slid back down the ladder like a fireman, and was running twenty yards up the trench to the next parapet to fire off two more before the snipers would know his position. "Chris! Aye, Chris. Come on Kit, tea's up."

Freddie Vickers stood looking down at Chris and could tell instantly by the look in his eyes, he understood as he had been there too. In 1916 it was called 'bottling it'. Today a more clinical term used is 'panic attack'. Freddie just waved a packet of Woodbine in front of Chris's face; he took one as if by instinct and pushed it between his cap and forehead. Chris then pulled himself up out of the trench ...and back into 1963. The flashbacks were still so real, but after nearly fifty years they had become a lot less frequent, thank God. Wiping the clay from his boots on a shovel standing in the spoil, he clumped across the road in his hobnail boots over to the canvas tent emblazoned with 'Chesterfield Gas Co'. He passed through the flaps and into the steamy interior, where five men sat on trestles around a large blacked aluminium kettle boiling away on the primus in the centre, and nearby, a folding table covered with enamel mugs and a split bag of Tate & Lyle. After its continuous dunking, the single teaspoon had grown to the size of a ladle.

"Are you going tomorrow?" asked Freddie.

"Yep. I am on duty so a free one, but I've got to take my two grandsons, so no bloody swearing or our Joan will play hell!" The St John Ambulance brigade was a very important part of Chris's life; he had joined up as soon as he had returned home in 1919.

It appealed to his sense of duty and he was always so passionate at being able to help others as much as humanly possible. For most of his

adult life he gave blood every six weeks or so, only stopping in later life by his doctor's insistence. He enjoyed the structure and camaraderie of 'St John's and progressed up through the ranks, and always looked so smart and splendid in his uniform and medals. It gave him pride and that semi-military comfort blanket he loved, especially the May Day parades and Armistice Day at Rose Hill where he would lay a wreath. He once appeared in the *Derbyshire Times* being inspected by Lady Mountbatten.

Grandad in St John uniform

Part of their weekly duties was to attend Chesterfield F.C. at Saltergate to offer treatment to any of the players, as broken legs, split heads and stud gashes where the norm in sixties' local football, so they provided a vital service. He would often take us, his grandchildren, who would sit behind the goal, and not inspired by the sport would play 'doctors' and wrap each other in bandages and slings.

After a second mug of tea and his packed lunch from a green and cream tin – a cheese and onion sandwich the size of a house brick and

Grandad on parade with St John Ambulance

a slice of Mother's fruit cake – he had another Woodbine and a look at the racing results in the communal *Daily Mirror*.

Several conversations were in full heat:

"…allotments, and how's your beans doing?"

"Moaning at being forced by their wives to help set up Mount Zion bring and buy."

"…football, that ref!"

"…the racing odds, and did you see him on telly?"

Suddenly they were interrupted by the tent flaps being thrown open. Silhouetted against the gap was George Poole, the foreman, in his rolled down wellies showing the white of the canvas, un ironed suit trousers, soiled gabardine and a trilby. "Come on now lads, if we don't get this done 'arf of Brampton won't 'ave any tea tonight and seeing as three of you silly buggers live there it's not a good idea."

Out came the men, all going through the motions, but inside wanting to be somewhere else. It was gone five when Freddie finished throwing a plank across the last bit of open trench, before pulling some black and white striped hurdles around the edge, one with a bold sign saying: 'Gas No Smoking'. He lit the yellow paraffin warning lamps and stood them around the hole. There obviously weren't many 'elfs' (Health & Safety Procedures) in 1963.

They all jumped up into the back of the Bedford truck, with its metal hoops and noisy canvas, men down the sides, tools in the middle, feet on top and headed back to the yard with the compressor bouncing along on the rear. In the early years, on a really bad day this would have taken him back too, looking down at the muddy boots on top of all the tools and fittings, they would suddenly morph into ammunition boxes and rifles. The engine noise, flapping canvas and the persistent clanking of the towing hook as though it was dragging an 18-pounder bouncing along behind, instead of a compressor. Plus, all the very familiar smells of petrol fumes, sweaty unwashed men and cigarettes, would add to the drama playing out in his head. It would only need an engine to backfire or a bawdy song to overload his senses. The truck often had to be stopped so he could jump down and be physically sick, leaving him to walk or catch the tram back to Brampton. The only cure was to get home as fast as possible, back to his world, his garden, and his beloved Frances.

"Not long now," thought Chris, a couple more weeks and that was him done, forty years' service digging and living in trenches for Chesterfield Gas Company. However, he didn't do much digging any more, he left that to the much younger ones. With his bad back and many years of experience, he was responsible for the cutting, threading and jointing of iron pipes. He had gone through all these emotions

Grandad's retirement from the Gas Works Co.

6

before, ever since he lied about his age to sign up in 1915, bureaucracy had followed him, and pensions had him recorded as two years older than he was.

They had tried to implement his retirement two years before, which I remember from the conversations I had heard as a child had taken some sorting out. It was going to be a big change; he would miss the banter for sure, the routine, the money, but most unsettling was that they would have to move home. Number 18 Alexander Road West was a Gas Company house that backed onto the Gas works at West Bars, which came as part of his job with a subsidised rental. Chris and Frances had brought up their two children there, Clifford and Joan, so it held many fond memories for them. They had registered with Chesterfield Borough Council and were awaiting their new first-floor flat: Number 11 Brindley Way, which was just being built on the new Pevril Estate near the site of the old 'Donkey Race Course'. When Chris was a child his mum and dad and ten siblings would all enjoy days out there as a treat on Bank Holidays, watching the races and enjoying the fun fairs and stalls. He had never imagined that one day he would be living there.

Rear of 18 Alexander Road and the modern Lidl supermarket

The truck rattled over the rail tracks as they entered the gate and came to a stop at West Bars depot. All out, tools away, the compressor pushed backwards into the shed for refuelling, then across the cobbles into George's office to clock off on the beautiful brass and mahogany Victorian time piece. As Chris walked up the yard old Sid emerged from his stores with a battered old watering can full of a foul liquid, no rose on the spout just a cork pushed into the end. Known as gas water it was a bi-product of the gasometers.

"That will shift the little blighters," said Sid.

"O thanks mate. I'll drop it off in the morning."

The scourge of damp terraced house cellars was silver fish and cockroaches, and by pouring this mixture around the cellar floor the insects would soon find another home, but the neighbours would show concern as they asked Frances about the strange smell. Chris walked to the top of the depot yard, jumped over the wall and down into his world: a neat garden full of flowers of every description.

He had a small lawn edged by curved bricks, and a winding brick path which led its way up past the privy and coal house to the back door.

"Ya can take those muddy boots off Chris," shouted Mother from deep inside, "I've just whitewashed that step."

Once inside, it was a strip wash at the pot sink with its two brass pillar taps, fitted with the latest fashion red rubber nozzles to direct the water flow. A mixture of Vim, sugar and Fairy Liquid was the only way to get his hands clean from the tanning in the flux and jointing compound he used. Hands now clean, but more like leather and sandpaper, he sat back in his chair by the range, slippers on, a 'fag' in the corner of his mouth and cup of tea in his hand. He checked the racing results in *The Star* newspaper, while Mother finished preparing tea of corn beef, marrow fat peas and boiled-to-mush 'taters'.

Joan in uniform

They heard Clifford coming on his BSA well before he turned the corner; their youngest was obviously calling in on his way home. They were very fortunate to have had both Clifford and Joan come through the second war, when they had close neighbours who had not been so lucky. Joan had gone into the 'Naffy' at Chilwell Barracks in Nottingham, and apart from the unwanted attention of randy GIs, had escaped unharmed.

Joan relished the freedom those years gave her, as the days of young ladies going off to university or cities on their own was unheard of pre-war. Clifford, an ex Tapton House boy who studied an electrical engineering apprenticeship, was kept in a reserved occupation as an armature winder at the BERL (British Electrical Repairs) on Lordsmill Street, so apart from aging with his forty a day habit and working 24/7, he too also came through unscathed. My Grandma Frances had been appointed as an ARP Warden, and with her tin hat and no-nonsense approach to open curtains during the nightly blackouts, had kept Brampton safe.

German bombers frequently passed right over Chesterfield heading towards the heavy industry of Sheffield, Forge Masters being one of their main targets, and it took quite a pounding. I remember she once recounted attending the crash site of a German Dornier, obviously hit by flak over Sheffield. It had turned away south, only to nose dive, crashing roughly where the two Loundsley Green Churches are now. But in 1940, it was described in The Derbyshire Times, as crashing over the gate, in the wheat field at the end of Greenback Drive, Ashgate.

Then there was Chris ...good old Chris. Always wanting to do the right thing, he had volunteered to join the ARP (Air Raid Precautions). This unit was based at the Congregational Chapel on Chatsworth Road, and they also had a medical post on Newbold Road, which he had to attend for further first-aid training. After being released from the Gas Works for the duration of the war he was sent for training in Lincolnshire, before being posted down to London to help in the East End during the Blitz, where he ended up staying throughout the war, finally coming home after the 'V' bombs had finished their reign of terror.

His gas repair knowledge served him well, but he primarily worked with St John Ambulance helping to look for survivors in bomb blasted buildings. It was two weeks on and five days off. Although he had always been known for his head of very thick brown hair. He returned after his first trip to the East End with it totally white from the trauma he had witnessed. Twenty years' previously he'd returned from Flanders still with his distinctive head of very thick brown hair, even after all he lived through and saw, so his experiences in the Blitz must have been truly horrendous.

The most vivid he recounted was entering a house, the windows and doors gone, and the adjacent homes flattened, only to find a whole family of Mum, Dad, two boys and a girl, all sat around a table in their Sunday best with a knife and fork in hand and not a mark on them, but all dead, killed by the high-frequency shockwave from the blast.

Clifford came in and threw off his leather flying helmet, scarf and gloves before placing his wax jacket on the back of the chair to warm. Chris offered him a Woodbine and Mother forced a cup of tea and a slice of fruit cake into his hand.

"Are you having one, Mum?" asked Cliff.

"I'll have one of my mental ones," she said, opening the drawer on the sideboard and pulling out a very sophisticated looking packet of Consulate menthol cigarettes.

Soon the room was full of a mixture of smoke and laughter, Cliff being a natural clown and lighting up the room with his smile. He had married Beryl and they had had two boys, Stephen and Andrew, so together with Joan and Jim's boys (Brian and David), that meant on a Saturday a house full of boys all under ten. It was so noisy, but to Chris it was also wonderful. With what had happened in those very dark days all those years ago, Chris knew he had made the right decision, but it still played heavily on his conscience.

Chapter 2

The Build Up, 1914

Christopher Loveridge was born on the 25th October 1897, the ninth child of David and Ellen Loveridge. After leaving school at 14, Chris (or his nickname 'Kit') had various jobs as a labourer. My mum told me for a short time he worked for Pilley's China Shop in Chesterfield as an errand boy. One day, however, he lost control of his barrow going down Goldwell Hill at Ashgate and all his pots got smashed and he got the sack. He then started work at a company called Robinsons who made pill boxes and lint bandages; their factory was literally over the road from number 86 Chester Street where he lived in a two-up two-down terrace with his parents and six of his ten siblings, the others having already married and moved away.

86 Chester Street

When he was very young, I believe about seven, he was taken seriously ill and suffered a mild stroke in which he lost the use of his right side and particularly his right hand, not permanently but serious enough to make him learn to write with his left. It took a good few years for him to convalesce enough for him to regain his strength to return to writing with his right hand. Combined with the taunting from his peers and siblings, the legacy was that for the rest of his life he became a very determined character, who was also ambidextrous. His party trick was to write equally elegantly in copperplate with his left and right hand, which as a young child myself who was just learning to write was really frustrating to watch. It was this dexterity and strength of character Chris had as a teenager that would manifest itself as a distinct advantage to him when it came to his use of weaponry later in life.

There had been a steady build-up of excitement in 1914 about the possibility of England going to war; the July newspapers were constantly full of the happenings across Europe, and it was all that Chris and his mates talked about. This was well before radios were widely available, so they read every newspaper item they could get hold of and watched cinema newsreels with total awe and disbelief. However, it was portrayed with a positive spin and the propaganda seemed to offer glamour and excitement compared with their boring repetitive lives in a factory. The feeling was that it was going to be over by Christmas!.There were posters everywhere on every boarding and noticeboard, all very convincing, putting a great pressure on these young lads to join up and "do their bit". Such was the need for more and more men, the army conveniently never checked the ages of these lads, thousands of whom were clearly no more than sixteen. Recruitment officers were paid handsomely: a shilling per recruit. So, you can

HAVE YOU A RELATION FRIEND OR SERVING?

Have you thought of giving him a hand by enlisting?

PARTICULARS FROM ANY RECRUITING OR ENQUIRY OFFICE

imagine they had no scruples and no incentive for turning these young lads away. There were many reported scenes of distraught parents dragging their underage offspring away, yet the pressure on these parents to be supportive of the war effort and deliver what the country was asking for was very intimidating. Charlie, one of Chris's elder brothers, was already in the Territorial Army when war was declared and so was one of the first to be enlisted. Ten years older and reputed to be a 'swanker' and show off, Charlie's home comings in his uniform with pretty girls on his arm set him as a role model for his younger brother. Then there was his constant taunting of Chris: "They would never accept a specimen like you".

Christmas 1914 came and went and although the news at this stage was not good the true reflection of what was happening over there was not common knowledge. There was still a buzz to be part of this big event, and a great social pressure that if you were young and healthy you were expected to sign up. So, Chris had made tentative enquiries many weeks before the 8th August 1915, after seeing a poster saying, 'Support your brothers in arms, sign up!'

Chris made his way into town to see the recruitment centre which had been set up at St James Hall on Vicar Lane (now housing the Low Pavement shopping precinct). Here, with officers from the Grassmoor Army Camp, he was part of a long queue that morning that wound halfway down Hollis Lane. Once inside, there was some basic paper-work to complete and he gave his age of 19 years 9 months, when he was only 17. He was then asked to pass behind a canvas screen where he had to strip off his shirt and vest to stand before a medic, who gave

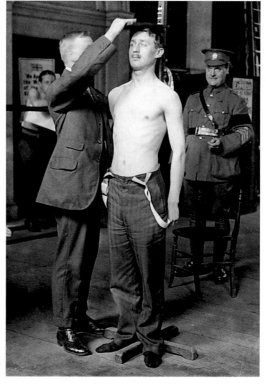

a cursory glance in his mouth, a quick check with a stethoscope as though to see if he had a heart, then it was over to an orderly with a white coat who took his chest size and other measurements, scribbling the detail diligently on a clipboard. He was listed as being 5' 3" tall with a 34" chest, so he must have looked very young and childlike.

Back out into the room, now dressed to stand in front of a very tall, rather rotund yet impressive looking uniformed officer, he was given a Bible to

PUBLIC RECORD OFFICE

WORLD WAR ONE SOLDIERS'
DOCUMENTS
WO 363

NEW SOLDIER'S
RECORD

Filmed by Microformat Systems b.v.
at the
Public Record Office.
The project is funded by the Heritage Lottery Fund
and the
Public Record Office

14

Renewals &c., which have taken place since Discharge.

[To be filled in when more than one award has already been made at the time that an Award Sheet is first taken into use].

Date of Award	Rate of Pension or Weekly Allowance under Art. 7 (1) R.W. 1918.		No. of Children under 16.	Duration of Pension or Allowance.	Gratuity.		Remarks.
	Man.	Children.			Art. 7 (1) R.W. 1917 or Art. 1 (3) R.W. 1918.	Art. 7 (2) R.W. 1917.	

Renewal or Revision of Award.

Name _____ Regt. _____ Code No. _____

MATTER NOW SUBMITTED. _____ Rep mid Bd. 12.9.19 _____

nil. M. P.

D.m.S. 4-11-19 — Bronchitis — aggrav. _____

	Init.	Date.	AWARD or DECISION.	Number of Children, and Allowance Granted.
Notifications to L.O. (P.F.) ...			Pension, Gratuity, or Weekly Allowance.	
A 1 9 to man ...		06.19.19	£5 - Supplementary - Gratuity.	3/- Chin 2/4/20
A 13 to N.H.I.C. ...			Continue current award to 8/fevered	
A ♈ to W.P.C. ...			Sept 3rd to nov: 4th 1919	
Record Card Completed		12" 19	Proposer's Signature and Date — Brjan 13.10.19	
Entered on S.B. 2. ...			Approver's Signature and Date H. Pereira 6.11.19	
Entered on Conditional List ...		13.11.19	Awarders' Instructions.	Initials and Date when issued.
			P.t. o. to notify wife.	
			P.t. o. 5.11.19	
Examined by F. Branch				

Pension Expires:— 4.5.20

DESCRIPTIVE REPORT ON ENLISTMENT.
(To correspond with Entries on the Medical History Sheet.)
Applicable to all ranks.

Name _Christopher Loveridge_

Apparent age _19_ years _9_ months.   Height _5_ feet _3_ inches.

Chest measurement { Girth when fully expanded _34½_ inches.
{ Range of expansion _2½_ inches.

Distinctive marks _Nil_

INFORMATION SUPPLIED BY RECRUIT.

Name and Address of next of kin _Ellen Loveridge   86 Chester Street_
Chesterfield   Derbyshire   Relationship _Mother_

Particulars as to Marriage.

(a) Christian and Surname of Woman to whom married, and whether spinster or widow. (b) Place and date of marriage.
(c) Present address. (d) Initials of Officer verifying entry.

(a)	(b)	(c)	(d)

Particulars as to Children.

Christian Names	Date and Place of Birth

STATEMENT OF THE SERVICES.

Regt. or Depot	Promotions, Reductions, Casualties, &c.	Army Rank	Dates	Service not allowed to reckon for fixing the rate of Pension		Service in Reserve not allowed to reckon towards G. C. Pay		Signature of Officers certifying correctness of entries.
				years	days	years	days	
towards limited engagement reckons from.			5-8-15					
Grassmoor			5-8-15					Jno St Quin Capt
19	Attested	Pte	5-8-15					Jno St Quin Capt
3rd B	Posted	"	5-10-15					Jno St Quin Capt
	Corps Transferred	"	7-4-16					
	Overseas	"	26-8-16					Derby W
	DISCHARGED ON DEMOBILIZATION March 1920					Transferred to Class Z Army Reserve on Demobilization Date 21 12 19 Signature Place At York N W Home Address 86 Chester St Chesterfield		
	in charge of G.C. Conduct							
	above			1	59			
	(date of discharge)			4	338	days		
				3	179			

(1947) W 9669—1673 500m 12/14 T. & W. Ltd.   27 Gen. No. 2325   Army Form B. 2505.

Duplicate

SHORT SERVICE.
(For the Duration of the War.)

ATTESTATION OF

No. *28827*   Name *Christopher Loveridge*   Corps *Sherwood Foresters*

Questions to be put to the Recruit before enlistment.	

1. What is your Name? ... ...   1. *Christopher Loveridge*
2. What is your full Address? ... ...   2. *86 Chatsworth Brampton Chesterfield Derbyshire*
3. Are you a British Subject? ... ...   3. *Yes*
4. What is your Age? ... ...   4. *19* Years *9* Months
5. What is your Trade or Calling? ... ...   5. *Miner*
6. Are you Married?   6. *No*
7. Have you ever served in any branch of His Majesty's Forces, naval or military, if so,* state particulars?   7. *No*
7A. Have you truly stated the whole, if any, of your previous service? ...   7A. *Yes*
8. Are you willing to be vaccinated?   8. *Yes*
9. Are you willing to be enlisted for General Service? ...   9. *Yes*
10. Did you receive a Notice, and do you understand its meaning, and who gave it to you?   10. *Yes*   Name *Sgt A. Down*   Corps *Sher Foresters*
11. Are you willing to serve upon the following conditions provided His Majesty should so long require your services?

   For the duration of the War, at the end of which you will be discharged with all convenient speed. If employed with Hospitals, depôts of Mounted Units, and as Clerks, etc., you may be retained after the termination of hostilities until your services can be spared, but such retention shall in no case exceed six months.   *Yes*

I, *Christopher Loveridge* do solemnly declare that the above answers made by me to the above questions are true, and that I am willing to fulfil the engagements made.

Chris Loveridge   SIGNATURE OF RECRUIT.

John H. Down   Signature of Witness.

OATH TO BE TAKEN BY RECRUIT ON ATTESTATION.

I, *Christopher Loveridge* swear by Almighty God, that I will be faithful and bear true Allegiance to His Majesty King George the Fifth, His Heirs and Successors, and that I will, as in duty bound, honestly and faithfully defend His Majesty, His Heirs and Successors, in Person, Crown, and dignity against all enemies, and will observe and obey all orders of His Majesty, His Heirs and Successors, and of the Generals and Officers set over me. So help me God.

CERTIFICATE OF MAGISTRATE OR ATTESTING OFFICER.

The Recruit above named was cautioned by me that if he made any false answer to any of the above questions he would be liable to be punished as provided in the Army Act.

CERTIFICATE OF MAGISTRATE OR ATTESTING OFFICER.

The Recruit above named was cautioned by me that if he made any false answer to any of the above questions he would be liable to be punished as provided in the Army Act.

CERTIFICATE OF MAGISTRATE OR ATTESTING OFFICER.

The Recruit above named was cautioned by me that if he made any false answer to any of the above questions he would be liable to be punished as provided in the Army Act.

CERTIFICATE OF MAGISTRATE OR ATTESTING OFFICER.

The Recruit above named was cautioned by me that if he made any false answer to any of the above questions he would be liable to be punished as provided in the Army Act.

CERTIFICATE OF MAGISTRATE OR ATTESTING OFFICER.

The Recruit above named was cautioned by me that if he made any false answer to any of the above questions he would be liable to be punished as provided in the Army Act.

CERTIFICATE OF MAGISTRATE OR ATTESTING OFFICER.

The Recruit above named was cautioned by me that if he made any false answer to any of the above questions he would be liable to be punished as provided in the Army Act.

CERTIFICATE OF MAGISTRATE OR ATTESTING OFFICER.

The Recruit above named was cautioned by me that if he made any false answer to any of the above questions he would be liable to be punished as provided in the Army Act.

CERTIFICATE OF MAGISTRATE OR ATTESTING OFFICER.

The Recruit above named was cautioned by me that if he made any false answer to any of the above questions he would be liable to be punished as provided in the Army Act.

hold and asked to swear "Allegiance to the King, his heirs and successors".

Then he signed his attestation papers where his physical details and next of kin information had been filled in, he was listed as a 'minor' as he was much younger looking than his declared near twenty years. He was then accepted without any further questions, given a full day's wages and sent away on unpaid leave and told to report back when notified.

As he headed back through the town centre, he thought everyone was looking at him as though he had done something wrong. Then he walked on along to West Bars and up Chatsworth Road towards Chester Street. As he walked, his emotions swung from panic: 'Oh God, what have I done' to the sheer joy that he had been accepted and could prove people wrong, especially Charlie, and that he too could be part of this big adventure.

So, it was with a mixture of pride and trepidation that he told his parents, my great-grandparents, David and Ellen. Deep down they had been expecting it but all knew it would turn out to be a life-changing decision one way or the other. Nonetheless, they encouraged him to believe that he was doing the right thing, and gave him their full support. He then lived in limbo for five days before being summoned to report back to St James Hall on the 13th August. Chris, and what seemed like hundreds of unkempt looking schoolboys, were marshalled into open back trucks and taken up through Hasland and along The Green to the camp at Grassmoor on the outskirts of Chesterfield.

On arrival, they were separated into smaller groups where, after a lot of shouting, they had to queue for what seemed like all day to have their hair cut and their feet measured for boots, before being handed underwear, kit and utensils, and various other uniform items. It was towards the end of the day, now kitted out in his khaki uniform, that he was billeted into a large bell tent with 12 other recruits, just like the numbers on a clock face, around a central Billy stove. Chris was surprised he was not the youngest by a long way; there was a tall farm labourer from Heath Village called William Hall who was just 16. The oldest in camp was 22.

It was brutal to be woken at 5.30am with Reveille (a bugle call to wake the soldiers and call them to duty) and sent outside for a strip cold wash and shave, a quick brew of tea whilst they tidied up, followed by inspection of their tent, bedding and themselves, before more shouting and being ordered to march around the perimeter. They were all out of step, looking more like a huddled mass than the British army, and after more intensive drilling they had to line up again for a scrutiny of their uniforms before being reprimanded for having muddy boots, even though they had been immaculate from the previous night's polishing, but now had become soiled by the early morning dew.

Breakfast was at 8.00am: two eggs, bacon, mushrooms, large slices of bread to soak up the lake of fat left on the plate, mugs of tea and endless cigarettes. This was better than home! Washing, cleaning and more marching until lunch, which lasted from 12.15 to 2pm, then more drilling and keep-fit exercises until 4.30pm; it was relentless. Often routines of various sorts continued until the final roll call at nine when you were dismissed and fell into their wooden frame camp bed and a deep sleep.

The routine and the repetitiveness made you act without thinking ...you were taken apart as a human being, the old Chris slowly disappeared, and you were put back together again as an army man. There was no time for any independent thinking, just reacting to orders no matter how repetitive or bizarre. The change that happened to all of them in such a short time was remarkable. They left camp, marching the four miles into Chesterfield. They had money in their pockets, looked smart and distinctive, and all were very proud of what they had become. As they entered the market place crowds watched as they were paraded, inspected, and then dismissed to enjoy their hard-earned five-day leave. Their families could not wait to see them and show them off to all their neighbours and friends. Girls smiled at Chris like they never had before, and men would part at the bar, slap him on the back and say, "Give 'em hell lad. You'll be back soon. Wish I was coming with you".

England had been at war now for nearly a year and it was slowly becoming clear that despite the bullish propaganda in the news the easy victory was not going to happen, the old ways and methods of battle had changed irrevocably. The early losses of the war had not manifested itself yet in Chesterfield, but in other towns the losses where truly horrendous. In one street in Manchester, the local priest knocked on the door of a terrace house to console and offer comfort to a newly widowed lady on the loss of her husband. As she opened the door she commented that it was nice of her neighbours to show their respect to her late husband by also pulling their curtains. Once inside, he told her that he had already visited six other homes opposite and the pulled drapes were for their loss not hers.

Chapter 3

The Change

Chris had undoubtedly changed in the last few weeks of his basic training; he had become a man and he relished being treated as one. Even his family called him Chris for the first time, and not "our youngen" or "Kit". His five days' leave had passed so quickly, it had been one big social whirl of friends and family, mixed with all the other personal things he had to do. He had spent a fortune in town buying things he thought he might need, silly things but this was all new and unknown, so he bought tinned treats, cough medicine, more woollen socks, plasters – what good they would do?

He had also queued up at Edna Seamen's photographic studio with all the other lads in new uniform to have photos taken, posing in front of a canvas backdrop, resplendent in khaki. His photo now took pride of place on the mantelpiece, the picture of his brother Charlie having been moved to second spot on the sideboard. Now there was a first!

Still up in the early hours ironing, polishing and packing, his father David sat in the rocking chair giving fatherly advice. Never having had military experience himself, it was all hearsay, but he did his best to reassure Chris and install a sense of duty, while trying to align all this to his strong Methodist beliefs. It all sounded at odds, but Chris agreed he would be a good soldier. After a couple of hours asleep in the other chair they both woke to Mother trying to prepare breakfast without disturbing them, but at the same time desperately wanting to spend the final hours with her 'baby'.

Breakfast itself was magnificent: kidneys, black pudding, eggs and proper thick back bacon with toasted bread. But it was quiet. Mother often nipped over to the sink to cry into her apron then it was hugs and kisses. She was too upset to come and wave him off, opting to stay at home whilst David helped Chris with his kit and walked with him along Chester Street and into town. The market square was cleared of all the stalls and filled with what seemed like hundreds of fresh-faced young soldiers all milling around, surrounded by wives and girlfriends. All the children had been given the morning off school, and everyone was smiling with pride and excitement whilst at the same time taking strength and comfort from each other.

Slowly the crowds parted and the men fell into lines, all marshalled by shouting sergeants with sticks, before the brass bands started up the military sound echoing around the square, then in from Beetwell Street came half a dozen cavalry led by the major on his enormous white horse, followed by another six on horseback, the black horses shinning like coal. Still mounted, the major made a rousing and often pompous speech, with many of the words being totally lost on these new recruits. This was followed by a blessing from the Bishop of Derby, with psalms and hymns. The men were then marshalled again into a line four abreast to follow the major and his cavalry along Burlington Street, Stephen's Place and down to the train station, with many a spit-and-polished boot falling foul of the horses as they marched.

The pavements were still lined with young boys, families and friends all shouting a mixture of "God save the King" and "Give 'em 'ell", mixed with tears and wails of "Love you, take care".

The procession regrouped at the station, the two awaiting trains filled the air with steam and smoke. Military organisation took over as the soldiers were all loaded into carriages, and with arms and hats waving from windows and doors, they pulled out of the station. Hoping to get a final view, their loved ones waved back from bridges, windows and embankments.

Then they were gone. Chesterfield fell eerily quiet, the youth and vitality leaving a huge void.

The pubs were Sunday-like, stands at Saltergate F.C. were half empty, and for the first time the world seemed full of only old men, women and children. The social effect was instant: jobs at Robinsons, Birtley and other engineering factories were offered to women of all ages and with no experience, such was the need for machined parts, pill boxes, lint and bandages etc. Sheepbridge works and another ammunition factory on Peverill Road, had also expanded into the lucrative manufacture of ammunitions. The original 'Chesterfield Cylinders' factory on Derby Road (where the cinema complex now stands) was punching out thousands of brass shell casings daily, so many local girls worked around the clock filling them with explosives.

Known as 'powder girls' or 'canaries', as their skin turned yellow, they became a very tight-knit group and were apparently quite a force to be reckoned with.

They must have been a tough lot, as the extremely strong chemicals had many widely damaging effects, not only on their skin colour but with their health in general. It was not uncommon for many to lose all their teeth, and anyone pregnant would miscarry, so these young ladies – many in their prime at only 16–18 years of age – sacrificed a great deal. Lots of these Brampton families now had money for the very first time, with the wives and daughters working and their husband's army pay being split 50/50 between them. It made a massive difference, unlike before when the family had to survive on what was left over when their man left the pub on a Friday night. Society was visibly changing in so many ways.

As the trains left Chesterfield it didn't seem odd to all who waved that they had gone north, not south towards the coast and France; the 3rd Battalion was to be kept in reserve, so had been sent north to be stationed at Darlington, part of the Tyne Garrison. To their loved ones they had gone off to war but their men were safe and enjoyed the excitement and adventure they had all signed up to. The Tyne garrison was going to be their home to complete basic training and many ended up staying there throughout the war. The camp was huge; as they pulled into the goods siding that night the lights of open braziers and oil lamps could be seen right across the horizon – set out like the Grassmoor camp but on a much bigger scale and with some more permanent looking timber Nissan huts.

They were organised to go to various parts of the camp, all carrying their kit and wooden supply boxes between two men, with rope handles that cut deep into hands. It was 10pm when they were finally billeted again into bell tents of twelve. Chris and William, the 16-year-old from Heath, had teamed up as they were the youngest and relished each other's support. They were awoken for a 5.30am start as usual, parading and marching, but this time there were lessons in every aspect of this new type of warfare: trench layout, why it was zig-zagged and constructed digging and reinforcing underground dugouts and communication centres. All types of shells and explosives, moving guns and machinery, bayonet charges and intense keep-fit.

The one thing they all hated was training wearing gas masks, as it was very uncomfortably, impractical and the thought of gas was the one thing that scared them above all else. Used by the Germans very early in 1914, it had had devastating effects not only in the field but more importantly physiologically. It brought terror, and with that came a hesitant soldier, which was the total opposite of what the British army trained these men for, and needed.

Then there was Chris's favourite: Lee Enfield rifles. They were taught to disassemble and reassemble without thinking, load and practice firing at various targets. The less attractive was the attaching of bayonets and being made to run screaming and charging at stuffed sacks of straw hanging from rope tethers. Unless this was done with absolute vigour and a fearsome drive they were made to repeat it again and again. Sometimes, it was only when the recruits were so angry that they imagined it was their drill sergeant they were attacking, that they then passed this test with valour.

Progressing on to the machine gun, Chris learnt with his other teammates to dismantle it quickly, then each carrying over 20lb of equipment, run, set up and fire on target time and time again. Many novices would think that because it threw out 600 rounds a minute it would be easy, yet they would still barely hit a target. But in the right hands – Chris's – it was an ultra-efficient weapon. He appreciated that by using it in short ten-second bursts there was less recoil so it was more accurate; it saved wasting ammunition and also kept the barrel cool so that it wouldn't jam. His right-hand man could then feed a constant stream of belted bullets 250 at a time (25 secs) making everyone count.

Chris was an absolute natural with just the way he held any type of gun, it felt as though it was part of his arm, and to the amazement of his instructors if he picked it up left- or right-handed he was equally as good. A combination of sharp eyes and his ambidextrous ability made him stand out, not only above his peers but his tutors too. There was a new experience of respect he had never had before, having always been made to feel like the sickly runt of the family. Now he was in a league of his own, and a well thought of marksman.

From day one the Germans had realised the full potential of machine guns, and with hindsight it is unbelievable that the British army only got around to setting up its own Machine Gun Corps late in 1915. One machine gun and its three or sometimes five-man team had the same fire power as forty highly trained riflemen. Invented in America by a Dr Richard Gatling in the 1860s, he came up with idea while he was at a firing range in Savannah, Georgia. Being frustrated by the constant gun recoil against his shoulder and then having to manually reload the bolt after each firing, he wondered if the two actions could be synchronised mechanically.

He achieved this, and his original machine fired an impressive 200 rounds a minute. It consisted of multiple barrels, each with an individual firing mechanism, with a top loading cassette of bullets rotating around a central crank. As the barrels were turned manually with a side hand crank, each barrel fired off a single shot. Cranked too slowly and it was inefficient, too fast and it would jam. To overcome this human error, later models were battery powered to give consistency of fire. Ironically, Dr Gatling's objective in creating this machine was driven by the hundreds of wounded soldiers that came across his operating table during the American Civil War. He believed that if by having such a machine it could mean a significant reduction in the number of fighting troops required in a battle, it would save many lives. Its initial reliability was inconsistent, so it still needed to be supported by a troop of riflemen. So initially it was more for a show of power than a truly effective battle field weapon.

The Gatling machine was then greatly improved on by a gentleman inventor called Ihram Stevens Maxim in 1883. Maxim was an avid well thought of established inventor, who also claimed to have invented the wire mouse trap and a single winged aeroplane way ahead of its time (which never actually flew). He took Gatling's firing pin gear mechanism and redesigned it, adding it to his new gun with just one single main barrel. His newly refined machine was now capable of throwing out 470 rounds per minute.

Seeking to promote his new machine to a global market, he very cleverly moved to London in 1885 and began a massive advertising campaign to launch his invention. His most ambitious slogan said that his gun would 'cut down a tree'. After inviting all the European Heads of State to watch, he performed many successful demonstrations of felling numerous twelve-inch diameter trees in Hyde Park. The orders and his subsequent substantial wealth flooded in. His name was now forever associated with his machine of mechanised human death, that could also be added to the billions of small mammals killed in his wire traps. Further refinement under licence by the British Vickers Company now added a water-cooled version to these machines, which, by the early 1900s, were now capable of firing over 600 rounds per minute.

At the height of the Battle of the Somme, it is reported that just ten British machine guns were fired continuously over a 12-hour period, sending out an astonishing one million bullets. At the start of the war in 1914, Germany's arsenal of their own designed version, known as the Maschinengewehr 08, or MG 08, were believed to be numbered at over 10,000 units, compared with only a few hundred of the British army's own Vickers machine.

The race was then on, and between 1915 and 1918, 1.1 million machine guns were manufactured between both these two great industrial powers and the USA. So, WW1 would end with Dr Richard Gatling's invention, designed to try and save lives, leading to 5.5 million soldiers being killed or wounded by these new types of machine guns. By being refined and developed further in the 1930s by an English inventor, Thompson, who stripped 60% of the weight away to give the more lightweight portable 'Trench Broom' or 'Tommy Gun' as they became known, they enabled troops to move easily, firing quickly and efficiently as they stormed enemy positions. These also became the weapon of choice for the gangster mobs of the USA and Italy, so prevalent at the time.

The subsequent modern-day machines, now fitted with lasers and capable of 1,200 rounds a minute, are still key to any battlefield engagement. These range from the ultra-lightweight semi-auto weapons, to the entrenched very heavy calibre ones.

Even Gatling's early invention has now been taken to the extreme, with the American GAU 8 Avenger 'Gatling gun' tank busting plane. It has ten, 8m-long, 27mm diameter rifled barrels that are powered directly from the jet engines. This causes them to spin at 3,000rpm and deliver 12,000 rounds in just 17 seconds, and because the barrels are rifled they can deliver 80% accurately within a 10m target zone. The enemy would not hear the bullets being fired as they travel at supersonic speeds towards them. If they did survive, they would then probably hear the scream of the twin jet engines racing to maximum power to counteract the massive recoil force of such a volley. Just one of these modern planes has the same firepower now as that of a whole battlefield of troops in WW 1. The cold efficiency of this plane was seen so clearly when they were used to devastating effect in the Gulf War against Sadam Hussain's retreating army.

Looking back at the old news reels of WWI, we cringe as we see the British soldiers being instructed to climb out over their protective trenches and walk in a straight single line, one man deep, head-on towards the enemy machine guns. This was not as inept as it looks; there was tactical British army logic behind it. With a single line of men, equally spaced, it meant there was more fresh air than human target for the German machine gunner to hit. Even if he only fired sweeping from side to side he would only (and I don't say 'only' lightly) hit 20% of the advancing force. The remaining 80% would get through and overrun the machine gun post.

However, this British tactic was quickly realised by the Germans, who then strategically repositioned all their machine gun posts to be able to fire on target, at the 'flanks' of the advancing troops. The military word 'flanks' referred to the sides, in the same context as when we say the flanks of a horse. This meant the line of men visible was much shorter so the line of fire was more concentrated, no arching through 90 degrees. It also meant the men would be walking at least 50 to 100 deep; therefore, each bullet fired could then inflict multiple wounds on more than one soldier, sometimes killing several with the same bullet.

The clinical efficiency of this type of fire saved bullets, which kept the gun barrel cooler so that it wouldn't jam when delivering yet more bullets. But, frighteningly, because of the deep concentration of human targets, it took the kill rate to 80%, with only 20% of troops getting through. A truly devastating consequence for the poor 'Tommy', used as just cannon fodder when told to advance, and why the sheer numbers killed, even in the most minor of skirmishes was, and still is, so hard to comprehend.

The most illustrative example of the machine gun's effectiveness was painfully learnt during the battle at Neuve Chapelle between 10th and 13th March, 1915. This was the first major battle of combined British and the newly formed Indian Corps, against the battle-hardened German 11th Jager Battalion. Despite poor weather, the British aerial recognisance pinpointed many of the strategic defences and the battle started with a massive Allied bombardment to destroy these fortifications. However, the British telecommunication lines were exposed and vulnerable to the elements; a failure in the British telephone system led to the initial barrage of the British heavy guns stopping early and short of their objective. Thinking that everywhere ahead of them was clear of enemy positions, 9,000 British soldiers were ordered to advance forward and take the previously held German positions.

However, after this initial bombardment there remained a mere ninety German infantrymen. That was a ratio of 100:1 British to German soldiers: outstanding odds for any British General. But unbeknown to the Allied forces, these stalwart few were holed up behind two remaining fortified machine gun posts. This small German unit laid down an overlapping arcing belt of fire on each flank of advancing British troops. It is believed some 24,000 rounds were sent across the battlefield. In the space of just ninety minutes, over 1,200 Indian and British soldiers lay dead, with the remainder pinned down and repulsed back into British lines. In the end, the only thing that saved the British force from complete and utter disaster was the resumption of the heavy barrage.

Finally, at the end of the battle, 21,000 men had been killed or injured. It is impossible to imagine these numbers on a page as they don't have a physical presence and don't mean anything to the reader. However, to try and put that into some sort of modern perspective of the sheer numbers involved, that is the equivalent of having all the 1200 staff and pupils at our local Brookfield School, rushing out at 3.30pm in the afternoon. If you then times that vision twenty-fold, so that's all the staff and pupils, times twenty, all sent to their deaths, just to be able to push the German line back by half a mile. That's Brookfield School to Morrisons; imagine the carnage of human debris left, on that length of Chatsworth Road. Claimed by the British as a clear victory despite their massive loses, this new pattern of warfare was now set, an entrenched stalemate.

The other striking fact for me that came from reading about this battle was that most of the Indian soldiers, who gave their lives so willingly, were never buried with the same reverence and recognition as the average British Tommy. To this day their sacrifice is not wholly recognised. This new ingrained way of fighting, which was so characteristic of the First World War, was also duplicated when Winston Churchill created a new Eastern Front at Gallipoli, to try and split the German resources. Here, very poorly trained, ill-equipped Turkish troops held the combined armies of the mighty British Empire at bay, pinned down on the beachhead with the help of just a few hundred, newly supplied German machine guns.

It was Sept 1915 when the British new purpose-built camp and training facility for its Machine Gun Corps (MGC) was set up at Belton House in Lincolnshire, just outside Grantham.

There the MGC recruited suitable men from all the regiments throughout the UK. As they had done with Chris, they looked at the top scoring privates, but these chosen few also had to have a very high level of IQ and intelligence, as well as being extremely physically fit.

The equipment was so heavy, with the barrel weighing 28lb, the water can 12lb, the stand 18lb, plus the boxes of ammunition at 20lb. They were recognised as the 'cream' of the army similar to how the SAS is seen today, so to be offered the opportunity to transfer into this new MGC was a great accolade, and one not to be turned down. So, after intensive training, Chris was offered a transfer and 6d a day extra pay (equivalent to £1 today) to become either a sniper or a machine gunner. It was a bit of a poisoned challis as in both options men had an average life expectancy of only six weeks. So, the fact that he survived and I can write his story is an amazing testament to his life. Preferring to work in a team, he chose to become a machine gunner

29

and was transferred to the newly formed MGC, regimental number: 30695, (as 120,000 joined up he was obviously in the first batch), Private Christopher Loveridge, roll number: 101b22, soon to be sent over to replace the losses in France that summer, which were horrendous.

The British army seemed inept at this new type of warfare and was very slow to learn from its early mistakes and predictability. Men were still being taught to walk while holding a straight line and not run towards the enemy, when speed and stealth could have won the day and saved thousands.

In October 1915, Chris was given a five-day pass and boarded a train south from Durham with twenty or so other Chesterfield lads who were also on leave. Chris returned home to Chesterfield, taller, stouter and a very confident young man; good food, exercise, and healthy outdoor living had made a massive impact on his well-being. In comparison, his peers still in the factory looked thin, gaunt and white from working shifts. David and Ellen were overjoyed to have him home and the same social parades to see friends and family took place. It was soon to be his eighteenth birthday on the 25th October, so that was very special too. Unbeknown to Chris, Charlie his older brother, was back from France, home on sick leave, having been shot in his left shoulder so wore his arm in a very polished leather sling, matching his belt and holster, it looked very smart. He too seemed different, showing a brotherly love that had always been vacant when they were growing up. Although never saying much to Chris about France, only chirpy banter, the look in Charlie's eyes spoke a thousand words.

For the first time also Charlie took his little brother for a pint, and as they walked along Chester Street they past two houses with curtains shut, which brought home the listings Ellen had shown them from the *Derbyshire Times*. They gave a cursory glance but didn't want to dwell. They walked to the end of the road, where there was a choice of two hostelries: the Royal Oak on the corner or the Bold Rodney across the road. Both sold a mixture of hearty ales, and the famous 'Brampton Ale' brewed just 200 yards away in a large impressive Victorian brewery (now home to two stores: Matalan and Wickes) shared its own rail track with the gas works (now a Lidl store). You can still see the chain halyards in the wall which were pulled out across the road to stop the traffic when the wagons were shunted in.

The only other reminder now of the old brewery is Spring Bank

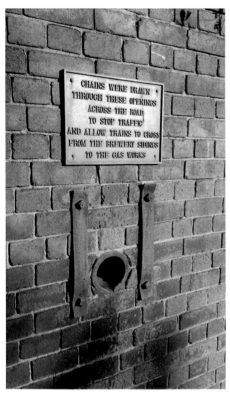

Chain halyard relic at the old gas works

Road, which supplied the spring water and the remains of the old rail gates at the bottom of Boythorpe Hill. Brampton Ale was regarded as one of the finest ales in the country, its secret ingredient being a local spring water, which not only made the mighty fine ale, it also gave it a slightly Epsom salt-ish side effect. As a consequence, regulars who drank it were extremely regular, to such an extent that if the miners and factory workers went away from Chesterfield on holiday, they had to take copious amounts of bottles with them or suffer the consequences of chronic constipation.

The Bold Rodney was open at five in the morning, to serve beer and breakfasts to both men clocking on and off from night shifts at the many factories, pits and engineering works dotted all around Brampton at this time. It also had some sort of 'traveller' association, the land to the side and rear often had smoky vans and tethered horses on it. In the summer, it held the sizeable Brampton Fair, where years later Chris would take Joan and Clifford, returning home with arms full of coconuts and teddies; Chris still being a crack-shot at the tin ducks and coconut shies was often banned by the stall holders as his reputation preceded him.

In contrast, The Royal Oak was a more refined establishment, run by the Chapman family (who had connections with my father-in-law) and as Chris and Charlie walked in together they were cordially welcomed, but not with the same enthused excitement Chris had been shown three months earlier. Turning around, they noticed George McDonnell sat in the corner – well 'perched' would be a better description. He had a large scar on his forehead, though not obvious at first, but it was the crutches leaning against the wall that made the brothers look twice, as did the one trouser leg pinned back, empty up to his waist. They made a fuss and chatted about everything but the bleeding obvious. They left some money behind the bar for a pint and a meal, then turned and sat by the fire.

Men like George, a plasterer and local footballer, what would they do now? Discharged with £5 and three months' pay, his future was not rosy, and over time the free drinks would dry up as he wouldn't be the only one disfigured sitting over an empty glass. Chris expressed his concerns to Charlie, which then gave him the opportunity to open up and confess to Chris that his army days also looked like being over too. He had another medical due in three weeks, and they were trying to find him an office job, but his office skills were limited and there was also intense rivalry for these safe desk jobs, 'the old-boy network' working in its mysterious way, and so, seeing George it had worsened Charlie's despair which he shared with Chris. He didn't want to alarm David and Ellen at this stage, but, they were going to be delighted that he would be safe and home for good.

The true extent of Charlie's injuries only became apparent the following morning when Chris came downstairs into the back kitchen to find Charlie shaving single-handedly, topless with his braces hanging down from his waist. Chris saw the red raw jagged scar twelve inches long running from his shoulder down to his waist. It had been stitched over and through just like a roast joint, obviously for speed, to close the wound with no time for cosmetic appeal. The neat 'nipple like' entry point he had shown David and Ellen, saying it was only a scratch, did not tell the devastating impact, as the shattered bone and bullet was forced backwards at 3,000 feet per second. They never said a word as Chris helped him back on with his vest, but it was clear to him Charlie's war days were over, and his mobility would be hindered for the rest of his life. This was quite a sombre moment for Chris; this wasn't a pumpkin or a turnip with an old colander as a helmet at 500 yards target practice that he was used to seeing. This was what a bullet did to a human being for real!

Charlie was eventually pensioned out the army at the end of 1917, and he bought into a Co-op Insurance round, which he developed very successfully. He married Jessie, and they settled at 525 Chatsworth Road, a small terrace at the end of Vincent Crescent. They never had any children, but I remember Jessie, who was a widow when I was taken there by my mum as a child, always kept a noisy caged mynah bird in the window.

After Jessie died, I remember it became a doctor's surgery for a short while, so it was strange to return there whenever I was ill. Charlie's left arm did remain quite weak and limp (how the tables had turned with him and Chris) but being right-handed he was able to compensate for his left side mobility and apparently became quite an enthusiastic tennis player. Often seen around Brampton in later years still looking very dapper in his whites and striped jumper, people commented that he still carried himself well, and with an air of confidence and pomposity.

The next few days were so good for Chris, not being brutally awoken at 5am. He relaxed for the first time in ages. He was enjoying Ellen's cooking and being able to do the normal things that he wanted to do was so appreciated. The weather was very mild for October, so Chris and his father went on long walks up over the fields to Linacre and around the reservoirs. This was a very special place for them both. David and Ellen were originally from Bishops Frome near Ledbury but had moved up to Chesterfield to take up the job offer as supervisor of the new filter and pumping station at the recently built Linacre dams.

Now retired from the Linacre dams he was still a water board superintendent. They had originally lived and brought their family up in a water board cottage, beautifully set in countryside away from the smoke and grime of industrial Chesterfield. The pair of semi-detached water board cottages was reached only by a footpath, and their nearest neighbour was Holme Hall Farm, where the public house is now. Here they had fields to play in as far as the eye could see; streams and lakes to swim in, with rabbits, pheasants and wood pigeons to catch, they had an idyllic, healthy and well-fed childhood.

Chris and his siblings attended school at Cutthorpe, walking over the fields carrying their packed lunches. The only downfall of this country existence was the six-mile walk into town on Saturday for market day, then walking back home six miles loaded with groceries. Apparently, they then moved in the late 1900s to a water board house on Sterland Street at Brampton and so the Loveridge children then transferred to the new Brampton Board School.

They moved again soon after, to 86 Chester Street, when his father was promoted to Superintendent. As they walked and talked in the late season sun it was delightful, sitting on the stone seat at the brow of the hill at Old Brampton, eating sandwiches lovingly prepared by Ellen and looking down on smokey Chesterfield, with the Crooked Spire poking just through the coal haze; the Great War seemed a world away, its true horrors were unimaginable to them both and yet they would soon be very real to Chris.

His birthday on the 25th October was special, all his relatives and friends were invited, and David presented him with a Bible to take with him. Handwritten on the inside front cover with pen and ink by my great-grandfather was the inscription:

Pte. Chris Loveridge. G. Com. 3rd Battalion Notts & Derbys
Oct 25th, 1915, his 18th Birthday, from Dad
"Be a good soldier and fight the battle of life and faith"

It said it all. Gone were the birthdays with trivial gifts of knitted socks, jumpers or fruit, this was so poignant. Chris would cherish this for the rest of his life; he took it over to France and then to Mount Zion every Sunday and eventually found great solace by clutching it so tightly on the day he died. It was eventually passed on to me from his daughter Joan, my mum, which after reading the inscription, inspired me to research his war years and try and understand what he went through to become the man he was.

Day six was a Monday: wash day. Ellen had sent Chris up to Mr Treece the baker on the corner of Bank and Charles Street to drop off a pie she had made the day before from the left-over Sunday roast. As a master baker, he would also put his neighbour's culinary efforts in his large bread oven for one penny an item. This was a time when all home cooking was done in the side of the range, so often on a mild day, not wanting to stoke up the range the fire wasn't lit to save the six penny-a-day coal it used. Often, like today, the coal would have been used to heat the copper, to boil the water and to help Helen cope with the hard labour of wash day.

It was while Chris stood chatting to Mr Treece, who had seen him grow from a sickly boy into the man he now was, that a pretty little thing with blonde hair in ringlets called Frances Boston floated in, also clutching her baking. They smiled, and after Mr Treece had introduced them, the conversation flowed, and flowed. Frances, originally from Bolsover, virtually told him her whole life story in detail.

She was working as a seamstress on Chatsworth Road and lived with her brother Jack, her mother and step-father, an ex-army sergeant, at 9 Brocklehurst Piece, Brampton. It was all going swimmingly well for Chris until she explained she already had a sweetheart called Charlie from Rotherham, who she wrote to and that he had gone over to France before Christmas to a place near Arras. Had he heard of it? Had he been over there yet? She was so anxious for news. He could see she was getting agitated and upset, he tried his best to placate her concerns, and as they parted he assured her she had nothing to worry about, Charlie would be back. As he walked home he cursed his luck in finding such a veritable beauty, that he could confidently chat to, and she lived in Brampton, but unfortunately was not unavailable…damn!

Chapter 4

The Machine Gun Corps

The ten days' leave just seemed to have evaporated, where had it gone? A letter arrived two days before with details of Chris's new posting to the MGC at Belton Park, with his departure from Chesterfield station at 10am on the Thursday morning. This time no market place parading or grand send-offs, just to report with his pass at Chesterfield station ready to go south. Saying his goodbyes were hard this time as they all knew he was going abroad not back up to the north-east, where the only dangers had been drunken Geordies on a Friday night out. David, his mum Ellen, Charlie and his youngest sister Nellie all came down to the station to see him off. The train was loaded and very busy, having stopped at Doncaster and Sheffield already, so space was hard to find as he pushed his way through to the window to give a final wave goodbye.

The train hissed clouds of steam and smoke as it pulled out of the station. He suddenly felt sick. The enormity of what he was doing washed over him and he began thinking of Charlie and George McDonnell's injuries, this was becoming very scary. He found a space and sat down, and as if the others could sense his unease the banter started, then the communal passing of cigarettes before the illegal hip flasks appeared. His apprehension faded and soon he was laughing and joking and enjoying the camaraderie of his peers. That was the thing about this war; they were all in this together, it brought people from all walks of life to become one big family. They were steel workers, farm labourers, grocery lads, telegram boys, office chaps and bank clerks, you name it; it was a complete cross section of society. Whether it was due to stress relief or the movement of the warm train, things quietened down, and Chris soon nodded off before waking abruptly when his head lolled to one side, only to then sit up and drift back into oblivion.

"Loughborough! Loughborough Station!" shouted the guard as the train came to a halt. This was his stop, ready to change over to the East Coast Line which would take him to Grantham. As he stood to collect his belongings the banter started again.

"Chris, you lucky bugger! Enjoy your holiday camp, we'll go and fight the bastards. There'll be none left to shoot by the time your lot get there."

With pats on his back and "Good luck, matey" ringing in his ears, Chris and several other lads on the train who had transferred to the new corps departed, waving to the mates he had just made as though they were long-lost buddies. That was it: with this war, relationships were made so quickly and so strong yet lost so easily. They changed platforms and began the slower rural train journey across country to Grantham. As they arrived, Chris and fifty or so other lads were marshalled outside the station and loaded into the back of several lorries, and with their kit bags in the middle, feet on top, they bounced along in a cloud of fumes. They made their way out of Grantham town in a long procession into the countryside and to Belton Park. Here, well away from the impressive stately Belton House in its extensive grounds, they found a newly built village.

No bell tents here, just rows and rows of long timber buildings, all painted white with asbestos roofs. There was even a Church of England Church, Roman Catholic and Methodist Chapels, dining rooms and kitchens, a YMCA central hall, medical and first-aid facilities. So, to be billeted into one of these new timber dormitories was sheer luxury. Each bed had a single wardrobe at the side and when not in use the

beds folded back 'futon' style to give more room for inspections and general living space. With the weather becoming colder these rooms were toasty warm from the two wood burning stoves, one at each end and draft free.

Life was looking good and was very different to the Tyne Garrison. They were all now true 'army men' and with their new-found status treated with much more respect by commanding officers. Life was structured, just like being at a public school, as they were set theory lessons using maths and geometry, which was interspersed with intense physical training and basic first-aid instruction and practical's using this new weaponry effectively, even wearing gas masks and basic first aid. They even had set times for lunch and evening meals, with free time to socialise in the YMCA hall, watch daft plays and listen to concerts, play games and write letters home.

The training was very physical, they were taught to run with the gun split into its three extremely heavy components: barrel 28lb, stand 19lb, cooling water 12lb, and ammunition belts with 250 rounds in boxes 20lb, with the three men moving at 20 yards apart so at least two might survive a stray shell or enemy gun fire. The later Vickers guns became air cooled, which made it a much easier piece of equipment to set up and carry, but with continuous use they tended to overheat. A lead gunner like Chris also wore a thickly padded shoulder canvas waistcoat, ribbed and stuffed with straw to enable him to sling the barrel (often hot) over his shoulder.

The Vickers machine gun

39

Establishing the gun station or 'nest' as it was called, required other heavy materials to be carried, such as angle iron which was to be hammered into the ground to support the corrugated iron sheeting formed at 90 degrees, before being dug out behind and the spoil thrown over the front to give slopping soil protection. The raised soil platform for the gun stand was covered with timber from ammunition boxes, and two slit trenches were dug out for the other two members of the team to be safe whilst the gunner fired on target. Being typically British these all had to be built in the same way and to the same specifications, any variation due to local terrain was frowned upon, regardless of there not being any flat fields in part of France, only a sea of undulating mud and sludge.

The machine gun station; gunners in gas masks, shoulder canvas

Well away from the camp – about a two-mile march down a winding country lane – was the enormous Peascliffe Rifle Range, comprising a semi-circle in a 600-yard radius of a timber balustrade ramped up with soil and turf at the front, a wide deep ditch behind to keep the target team safe, and then backed by an even higher earthen wall to catch any stray bullets. The cardboard bull's eye targets were attached to what looked like mechanical bicycle parts with a chain driven system, which meant they could be raised and lowered to be checked for their individual accuracy, with the corps' results then being telephoned back up to the commanding officer and his men 600 yards away. (The arched banked earth wall is still there today, now heavily wooded and part of a luxury golf course, with the off-target bullets clearly visible, coming to the surface.) Sometimes the country lane was closed off at both ends by the military police, so the snipers and machine gunners could practise firing at the targets from over a mile away.

Chris was very happy, he had made some good friends and his life had real structure: he was well paid, well fed and extremely well looked-after, medically speaking. No paying sixpence into a medical scheme here, he had free access to the army doctor and dentist. They were even allowed passes into Grantham for the occasional night's freedom, with a few beers, a dance maybe, and lots of pretty girls; the draw of men in uniform with money to spend brought lots of girls into town, some not as innocent as others. In fact, the very first woman police officer in England was a lady called Edith Smith of Grantham, who was set on primarily to deal with the problem of 'ladies of the night' who tried to solicit directly outside the camp gates.

As winter approached and Christmas 1915 drew closer, Chris knew his overseas posting was imminent, so he was so relieved to have one more Christmas in the UK, at home on leave with his family. He had completed his basic training and now had his full MGC insignia. Many of the men he knew when he first arrived had already been shipped over to France, and such was the constant flow of men he found he was spending much of his time helping teach the new recruits. It came as no surprise in early spring 1916 when he and about 200 other men were summoned into the YMCA hall. The issuing of badges and awards for marksmanship and other promotions took place, followed by the news they had all been hoping they would never hear: they were going over to Belgium the very next day.

There was an immediate letter embargo, so no last contact with home to let them know what was happening, it was literally "Pack your stuff, here is a check list of equipment you need to collect from the stores, report here at 0600 hours tomorrow morning". That was it, no pomp or gallant speeches this time; they were now just a small cog in a very big production machine. They had been given the best equipment and training the British army could offer. It was now down to them to be a team player, support their peers, prove themselves, and with a fair wind and good luck they might come home.

The morning was very cold and white with frost, so to have to leave

41

a nice bed and wood burners (till God knows when) and march out onto crisp, starched grass and seem enthused, was tough. There were twelve lorries; eight men sat on either side with others in the middle on kit bags, and with the flapping canvas sides, extreme wind chill and feeling every bump in the road, they left the camp and headed towards Grantham and the station. All out, they were relieved to be able to stretch legs and stamp feet to get warm, many surging for the limited facilities to complete their ablutions, a mixture of fear and body clocks. There were volunteer ladies on the platform dispensing mugs of sweet tea and bacon baps, which were well received.

As the train arrived and the steam cleared to everyone's disappointment, it was made up of low open goods wagons. Obviously used to transport all things agricultural there was nowhere to sit, so they all stood in these open carriages for the thirty minutes across country back to Loughborough. Wind chill took on a new meaning, as just like penguins, they took it in turns to move around from the front and edges back into the middle to stay warm, the only relief was the occasional downdraft of steam as the train passed under bridges or struggled up gradients. Straight into the goods yard at Loughborough, they dismounted onto the gravel and then marshalled two abreast 300 yards over the tracks and up onto the platform. Here they were met with other men in uniform from all over the UK. On board another train with yet more soldiers crammed in, they settled back down for the next leg down to Marylebone Station in London.

As the train pulled into Leicester Station to collect even more troops, pulling into the north platform parallel on the adjacent track stopped another train. This time there were no smiley faces, no waving arms and hats hanging out of windows. It was full of sedate bandaged men, some sitting, but most lying on stretchers across seats. Nurses in white uniforms and hats could be seen walking up and down the corridors carrying trays, bowls and dressings. There were no smiles or banter from any of them, just a starry-eyed look. The orderlies carried them off the train and into waiting ambulances, even some flat-bed lorries, and horse and carts.

Leicester was one of the major medical centres set up to cope with the returning influx of these much-damaged people. The need for hospital trains had been a priority from day one, and the response from the public to raise money and come to the aid of the individual railway

42

networks was very impressive. Like the great civilian fundraising in WW2 for Spitfires, there was enormous local pride that people could do their bit for these returning heroes. So, local townsfolk with their dignitaries were proud to be photographed alongside newly resplendent hospital carriages. The St John organisation really came to the fore, for example, working with the Lancashire & Yorkshire Railway, as with their help and sponsorship they really made a difference.

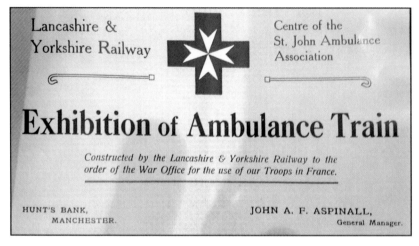

It was August 24th 1914, when the first group of 111 casualties arrived back at Southampton Docks, to be taken to Netley Hospital on a War Department train kitted out with triple bunks and extra first-class carriages for the walking wounded.

As the number of returning hospital trains increased, the powers that be always tried to plan them to arrive under the cover of darkness and were keen to keep the arrival time a secret. But word would get out and crowds of people would gather to cheer them home with flags and bunting. However, there were many families who came to vainly look for their loved ones who had been reported missing at the 'Western Front'. The local newspapers had a field day listing the exact numbers that had returned, and always commented on whether they were on a stretcher or part of the walking wounded. They often showed photos of soldiers with descriptive details of their injuries and got them to tell their reader of the experiences, "over there" always written up with a positive spin. This was initially frowned on by many newspapers, but as readership numbers were everything they all eventually followed suit.

Interior of an ambulance train

Obviously as the number of casualties grew the government tried to suppress access to the exact amount, not only for the well-being and morale of our home front, but also as this knowledge could prove great PR information for our enemy who could then assess how their tactics had worked. By the end of the war there were 3,982 ambulance carriages of all types and refinement in service across the British rail networks, and the total numbers transported of all the sick and wounded, including often the German injured and now prisoners of war, totalled 2,680,050; a quite outstanding logistic achievement.

This train had a sombre effect on all the men on the train as they looked across into the Hospital carriages. So; they were all quite relieved when their train started to move out of Leicester to continue its journey south. "Chaos" was the only way Chris could describe it: troops, thousands of troops from all parts of the UK and abroad, all milling about in and around Marylebone Station. The lorries –he had never seen so many, not even at Robinsons – were stacked with crates and boxes, towing trailers, all trying to go in the same direction. The soldiers eventually escaped the train yard and station and were marched across town to their next train from Victoria. Grabbing handfuls of sandwiches as they passed the lady volunteers on the platform, they were ushered and pushed onto the next train with yet more bags and equipment. It really was crammed this time, some men even escaping the seating into the luggage racks above, to make the slow rock and roll exit out of London, into the countryside and down to Dover.

They arrived at the dockside that night and were marched straight onto the waiting transport ship, where they were fed hot food before looking for a place to bed down for the night. Another early wake up call with tea and breakfast, with most men on deck having their first Woodbine or Park Drive of the day, busy looking at the harbour in daylight, with a heavy feeling and a cursory glance out to sea and across the channel.

Over on another pier there were horses, hundreds of them, breath steaming in the cold morning air, all being man-handled and marshalled reluctantly through straw-bale-lined walkways, up the gangplanks and deep into the ship's hold. The straw bales were then collected and lifted on board with the steam winches. For every horse loaded there seemed to be the same number of men, all responsible for the welfare of the horses assigned into their care. This boat was due for Gibraltar on its way around to the Mediterranean.

I can remember my father's uncle, Pte. Tom Fletcher from Boythorpe, telling me stories of WW1 when he took horses on a similar trip during his time in the Great War. It certainly wasn't a pleasure cruise; there was a real fear of German U-boats, rough seas in the Bay of Biscay, and sea-sick, distressed horses with no exercise or daylight for two to three weeks – the stench! These ships could be smelled way before they came into any port. These were chartered cargo ships, so no provision for ventilation had been designed in them for their traditional static cargos. Therefore, with next to no clean air below decks and mediocre mucking out, it was truly horrendous. Many of the horses, despite best efforts, literally died where they were standing, and to remove them deep within the ship's hold they had to be butchered where they lay and then tipped overboard.

It was 1100 hours when the steam whistle blew; the ropes were thrown over the side and the ship, loaded with thousands of fresh-faced troops, moved slowly out of the protection of the harbour wall, turned and headed over to Boulogne. The risk of U-boats was very real; men on every vantage point seemed to be staring through binoculars for any glimpse of a periscope trail, the gunners were moving guns in 90-degree arcs ready for that one 'shout' they hoped they would not hear. As the White Cliffs grew smaller in the far distance, the tension on board was palpable, 90% of these men had never left their county never mind their country so it was all strange to say the least. When on the horizon the French coast came into view, there was a sense of relief to be safe from any U-boats, but anxiety for the next leg of their journey was growing, manifesting itself in raucous banter and over-exuberance as they looked at each other for support.

As the ship joined a long queue to disembark its cargo of troops and equipment it was nearly dusk before Chris and the other soldiers were fed and allocated bell tents for the night in a massive camp, one hour's march from the docks. The next two days they rested, had time to write home, clean and prep their clothes and equipment. On day three, army logistics took control, separating and identifying who was being transported out first. Some were marched out; some lucky ones were transported by London buses, flat-bed lorries and open charabancs. Chris and his MGC pals were sent by train to a camp at Chamiers, which was the French equivalent of Belton Park. Here they were all issued with new equipment, and when not studying maps and geometry, they had more intense physical training and target practice. They camped here for a further six days before being split into groups and allocated to various platoons along the front line, which now stretched from the Belgium coast to the border with Switzerland.

Chapter 5

The Reality

It was very late when they piled into the support trench; they sat with their backs towards the Hun. Pushing their bodies hard against the mud walls dug into the side of the trench, they tried to sleep. It was a pitiful respite, and everyone was on edge and restless. There was the constant odd gun fire, flares lighting up the sky, lots of shouting and then the intense damp and cold which made sleep almost impossible.

One chap, a tall cocky lad called Sid who was always winding everyone up with his jokes and rude banter, stood up to light his cigarette. As he lit it, the light attracted the German sniper who had been half asleep under his soil covered tarpaulin. Sid passed the cigarette to his mate. The sniper took aim. As Sid pulled his hand back to blow out the match, a shot rang out. His helmet sounding like a Church hand bell, Sid fell backwards against the trench wall and slid down into the mud and sludge. German snipers knew these fresh troops coming into the trenches for their first time were easy pickings, a time when they could 'make hay' in these first few days.

Chris in a forward trench

So many young men not heeding warnings from the 'old hands' and being naively curious, they would literally want to look over the side into no man's land, only to be taken out with the first bullet. Sid was the first casualty the men had witnessed at close range. They sat staring at his corpse, no-one moved at first. The men just shut their eyes then reopened them as if to see it was real. After what seemed like an eternity they were all awoken fully by an order to 'Stand-To'. It was a while before Chris noticed that Sid's muddy remains had been spirited away, but as he must have slept he hadn't noticed by whom.

Stand-To was always an hour before dawn, those that were sleeping were woken up by the company orderly officer and sergeant. Everyone had to fix bayonets and take up positions along the trench to guard against a dawn raid from the enemy. Even though they were further back in the support trench there was still a possibility of a breakthrough and attack. Both sides had the same routine as they both knew dawn was the time each was likely to start any new offensive. Every British soldier knew that usually the cessation of enemy artillery bombardment signalled the onset of an infantry assault. If, however, this didn't happen, as light grew the routine continued by what was known as the 'morning hate'. As if by clockwork both sides would fire off machine guns, shelling and random small arms fire at each other, as if to say, "we are still here" and establish their territorial rights across this muddy field. Many a man was caught out by a random bullet or shell as he concentrated on his morning ablutions.

As quickly as it all started it would fall silent as both side were 'stood down' to have breakfast – all very civilised – both sides creating a routine not wanting to agitate the other. Breakfast was brought up in containers from distant field kitchens, so it was often tepid at best. This morning it was a strange looking stew with fat pooling on top as it slowly congealed. It was probably the soldier's standard tinned meat issue called 'McConachie', topped up with whatever local vegetables they could find, and often horse meat.

The British army had long realised the old saying 'an army marches on its stomach' was very true. The energy sapping physical exercise, cold outdoor living, plus the draining of constant adrenaline meant that these men needed twice the normal daily intake of the suggested 3,547 calories per day. At the start of the war the soldiers' rations were plentiful and were specified to be 10oz of meat and 8oz of vegetables per week, to be split into daily rations. This was only managed on average nine out of thirty days, so McConachie was the army's proven simple way of feeding the troops.

Supplied in small pocket-sized tins, it was loaded with masses of fat, meat, turnips and carrots. It could be eaten cold, with the lid rolled back, and was white with congealed fat surrounding the coarse chunks of meat and vegetables – similar, perhaps, to a tin of corned beef mixed with vegetables and surrounded by lard. Obviously it was preferable to be served hot, often warmed by a candle or on a mess tin or a fuel can with charcoal, as it looked and tasted far more appetizing. It was always accompanied with the standard issue Huntley & Palmers Army No.3 biscuit. These were so hard they were teeth breaking, and could only be consumed by soaking first in hot tea, cold water or in a warm stew. They were in fact so hard that even soaking them overnight made hardly any difference, so many soldiers ground them into pieces with a stone to try and make flour which they could add to a stew.

Trench food was bland and monotonous to say the least, and barely gave what was intended to give these poor lads the high calories they needed to survive. Scavenging became a focus of life, and wherever they marched they all looked out for that lost farm animal, field vegetables or any abandoned houses they could pillage – any little extra to top up their rations and give them a variety.

The Royal Mail post was an absolute lifeline to these young lads. It was an unbelievably efficient service given the conditions, and so packages from home of fruit cake, home baking and tinned goods poured into the trenches, to be opened with excitement and always shared with fellow comrades. Harry Patch, 'The Last Tommy', who was also in the MGC, spoke so passionately about the camaraderie with his little team of five. They literally lived in each other's pockets, slept under the same blankets to keep warm, and shared all the same fears and emotions. It was with relish they looked forward to the parcels from home, with the plethora of food and dry home knitted clothes etc., sharing them equally amongst the crew. Even sharing pairs of socks so two people could at least have one good one each. Like Chris's experiences,

Harry Patch's own nemesis came one day in September 1917 when he and his machine gun crew were typically walking twenty yards apart, as trained, back from the line, when a passing shell burst above them killing all but Harry. There was nothing ever found of his 'brothers in arms', which traumatized him so much. Although wounded, he survived to tell his amazing stories later in life. Like many returning unsung heroes, he never mentioned any of his war years, not even to his wife and family. He returned home to become a plumber, blocking out 'that day' completely, only being comfortable to open up and speak to a local radio station as the 75th anniversary became public interest, which in turn led to his amazing book being published. Reading it encouraged me to find out about my own Grandfather Chris.

At breakfast time, half the men would eat whilst the remaining would either keep watch or clean their weapons, and they would then all change round for the second shift. When all were fed there would be an inspection by the platoon officer and sergeant. Their main concern was the cleanliness of the soldiers' weapons, not so much the soldiers themselves. They looked to make sure their uniforms, though often very dirty, were still fit for purpose, and they paid particular attention to look for signs of trench foot, so the order to remove boots and socks often made these inspections look quite comical. Inspection over, the platoon sergeant and corporals would then assign daily chores to each man. This could be anything from being put on watch for two hours at a time, or filling sand bags, digging out any shell debris and repairing the trench sides, pumping water out of the bottom and cutting new duck boards to walk on to keep feet dry.

The less attractive chores included emptying latrines and digging new ones, but generally it was just keeping the trench in good order so that men could work and move safely below the parapet. Daylight meant that movement should be kept to a minimum, so the rest of the day was often one of utter boredom. Keeping low in their safety zone cleaning weapons, eating, trying to wash and shave, writing home, and preparing somewhere nice and dry to snatch any sleep they could before night time.

With the light fading and the onset of dusk Stand-To, the repeated ritual of fixing bayonets took place, with everyone taking up their allocated positions just in case there was an evening raid. Again, random shells and shots would be exchanged with each other before it all fell calm and the night time resupply could begin, with men moving massive amounts of ammunition, timber, tools and materials along the feed trenches up to the front. Self-absorbed in their tasks, men would be taken by the sudden flash of a flair followed by the seemingly simultaneous rifle fire.

It was a constant war of attrition from both sides, all the intensive training to make men into efficient fighting machines often came down to just bad luck of being in the wrong place at the wrong time. Chris spent the first week in this support trench with every day being much the same, disappointed that he was not able to use the skills in which he had been trained. The days were very cold with the sun barely melting the frost before it froze harder again the next night. Music and singing would waft over from each trench, as if both sides were trying to reach out, grasp normality and make sense of what was going on.

That night at Stand-To, Chris was ordered to gather his belongings and move up to the front line with about fifty or so other men; from the whispers he had heard there was going to be an attack on the enemy line in their sector very soon. Chris, Arthur and Pete, who had been separated on arrival, now found themselves back together in the original team from MGC Belton. This gave them a boost in confidence; it was as if, by magic, the British army had worked in its wondrous way.

They waited until about 2am, when, under the cover of darkness, they all moved slowly and carefully in a long snake-like procession, carrying their own equipment and lots of other supplies. It was difficult to pass by the men huddled, trying to sleep on clay shelves cut into the sides of the trench, often catching them as they passed, then hearing the words "Clumsy bastard" as the pile of tarpaulin and blanket raised itself then resettled back down. The noise as they moved forward steadily grew too, this wasn't random gun fire it was a continuous noise of shells, gun fire and passing bullets. Both sides had to cover the sound of men and equipment moving forward, making it more active sometimes at night than during the day.

It was 4.30am when they arrived and settled down for literally a catnap before Stand-To was called again, with its usual routine performed, but this time there was no mistaking how close to the German trenches they were. It sounds silly, but sometimes the nearer you were to the German front lines often the safer you were, as the Germans and likewise the British, would not want to hit their own trenches with shells. So, you frequently saw and heard them whoosh past overhead, each side targeting the supply trenches set further back.

Chris, Arthur and Pete were taken into an underground bunker by the platoon sergeant where they were shown a map of the trench position they occupied. To the left-hand side was an already established machine gun nest, of which they were instructed to relieve the existing crew. So as soon as the 'morning hate' was over they made their way slowly, quietly carrying ammunition and supplies, along the narrow slit trench to the raised abutment where the nest was established. On arrival, they were silently greeted by three very weary, very dishevelled looking men. They showed Chris a map highlighting their present position, and 'Jerry's' front line. Then using field glasses and a periscope they were shown the narrow gulley where Jerry would try to push through if he were to make an attack towards the British front line. That was it, the crew were gone.

Chris, Arthur and Pete nervously started to settle in and tidy up things as best they could without drawing attention to themselves. While one kept watch with the gun, the others filled old ammunition boxes with earth to reinforce the area around the parapet then filled sandbags to make a safer area to try and sleep later. As Arthur watched and covered them with his Enfield, Chris and Pete cleaned and oiled the mechanism of the machine gun and prepped the ammunition. This was the hardest bit; they were very scared, their nerves on edge. It was the not knowing that made the adrenalin run through your veins and sometimes even down your leg.

For the next two days they watched diligently, taking it in turns to eat or catch up on some sleep. They felt very isolated and cold. It was frosty and during the day often snowflakes fell and were quickly absorbed into the mud. It was just after the morning Stand-To, they had finished breakfast and the boredom of another day was just starting to take hold. Pete saw them first. Five, maybe six, men creeping towards the gulley. Without a word, Chris pointed and adjusted the sight of the machine gun. Arthur lifted the belts to give an easy flow of bullets. They looked at each other, nodded, and Chris pulled the trigger for the first time in anger. It seemed surreal as he watched the six men crumple and slide to the floor. With a cold sweat running down his forehead, and visibly shaking, he threw up all over his arms and onto the back of the gun, where his vomit sizzled from the heat. Before they had time to think, the German snipers were on them, hitting the bags and splitting boxes they had filled when they arrived, sending deadly splinters all around the trench.

That was the consequence of operating a machine gun: you may as well wave a red flag saying, 'we're here'. A trained sniper was trained to shoot, move, shoot again, making the opposition believe there were several with him. They all knew they would be safe for the next thirty minutes or so, and then if the sniper couldn't get you, the German artillery would try. Just one shell bursting overhead would be all that was needed to take all three men out. Still staring with unblinking cold eyes, they saw more movement, so Chris let burst again as he saw head and shoulders come above their parapet. How many more are there? What are they waiting for? Was this just a little push to probe defences, or the start of something bigger?

Minutes seemed like hours. Their eyes ached through staring at the featureless landscape looking for anything that may give a clue. They all agreed they would be better if they could move further along to the next abutment thirty yards to their left. They would have a clearer view and better protection. Chris gave cover with his Enfield, firing whenever he thought he saw movement, while the other two men moved the gun, stand and ammunition boxes, and whatever supplies they could carry.

Now reassembled and better protected than before, they watched as snipers still fired onto their old position. With this new view they could clearly see the jumble of bodies from before. Their hunch was correct. Three shells suddenly burst, tracking in a perfect arc over their old position, still powerful enough to blow a load of mud and debris all over them. But they were unharmed. Again, it happened so fast, obviously the Germans thinking the shells had just taken them out, twenty maybe thirty men now moved calmly forward towards their right-hand side.

"Ready," said Chris, "wait till they get to the old cart wheel." Then, like robots, they opened fire in ten second bursts...let the smoke clear...check the belt fire again. More men were piling over and out through the gulley. As some fell others fell on top and yet more came forward. The Germans seemed unsure where the fire was coming from as Chris kept firing in a 30-degree arc into their flanks. Chris watched as they fell awkwardly, sometimes spinning around like a ballerina as the force of the bullet hit them.

The sound was strange too. It was a mixture of a dull thud and torn rags as the bullets ripped them apart. The worst thing was the men groaning and writhing on the floor, and then their cries and shouts, which often carried on for hours. Many were left there shouting for their 'mutter', others lay with their stomachs torn open, shaking and making the most unearthly sounds. One man was clearly dead, but his half-severed leg twitched involuntary like that of a school biology frog or a dead headless chicken.

In the trenches often slightly wounded soldiers would, unbeknown to them, have become infected by their environment. Naively they were deluded that their injuries weren't going to be fatal. Maybe injured a couple of days before, they believed the dressing had done its job and the pain was now receding and they felt so much better. In truth, they had only gained a strange out-of-body numbness and an awful complexion which came shortly before death. Firing back and forth towards their exit point, Chris kept his finger on the trigger until he saw no more were coming through. After catching the odd straggler out in no man's land he stopped and looked. It then fell silent.

This time there was no incoming sniper fire. Scared to believe what had just happened, and that they had been successful, it was only then they saw the devastation caused by this hot, oil smelling machine in front of them. Looking at each other, but not saying a word, they had all just changed irrevocably. No amount of Wesleyan Church upbringing or army training had prepared Chris for this alien feeling. Holding his Bible tightly in his hand he kept saying the Lord's Prayer, over and over again, as he tried to make sense of this new life order he found himself in.

Christmas of 1916 had long gone. In the end there was no big push from either side. All offensives used a tactic called 'push and bite', where each side would shell the front position in an arc, then push troops forward to take a 'bite' out of the enemy line. Their instructions were then to hold and defend it against any German counter-attack. The only flaw in this tactic was that you now had enemy forces not only in front of you, but on both of your flanks. So, it was often only a matter of time before the 'gate' was closed behind you, and you were either taken prisoner or this new hard-fought ground was lost, so you retreated, leaving many injured and dead behind, only then to be forced to retake it again a couple of days later.

The weeks and months blended into each other, each day and week it was the same routine, only broken up with the odd skirmish and with very little respite. Known as the 'Trench Cycle', it was two weeks in the front line, one week in a support line, then another two weeks in reserve and finally one-week rest. Like all people, in say the police and medical professions, often a dark humour takes over to make death seem a normal part of life. Even Chris was becoming accepting of it and the slow transition that shooting people as a day job seemed a perfectly natural thing to be doing.

February 1917 was a particularly cruel winter and it caught him out one night as he slept. After his two-week cycle at the front he was relieved to be further back in a support trench, being relatively quieter, where he fell exhaustedly into a deep sleep. He must have stretched his leg outside from under his blanket and tarp, as he woke up in the morning with a feeling that could only be described as having a lead weight and a red-hot poker in his shoe. Looking down he could see his boot was covered with white frost, and having no control over his ankle or foot, had to remain seated at Stand-To. Sent back down the line to a medical station, hobbling and with the help of a stretcher-bearer, he found he wasn't alone in his anguish. The medic cut the side leather and removed his boot and then his frozen sock which was stuck to his skin, only then could they see the left side of his foot was badly discoloured, like a red frozen chicken.

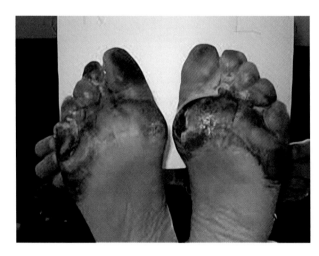

Severe frostbite to the feet

The first thing the doctor did was to push a large needle into the affected part of his foot, this was to check the depth of frozen tissue to see if was 'frost nip', just the top layer of skin, or the more serious 'frost bite', which in worst-case scenarios would freeze right down to the bone and cause gangrene. Chris felt nothing, so it was serious. It was also the army's way of sorting the malingerers out from the truly needy. Chris had his foot bathed and bandaged before being sent further back down the line on a hospital trolley. These crudely constructed, wooden, double-decked trolleys, often run on wooden rails, were pushed by other troops not on operational duties.

Hospital trolley

These were needed to get the injured to a branch line where they could be transferred to a returning ammunition train on its way back to the field hospital, set well back from the front. As they approached the hospital, off to the side Chris could see a large pile of what looked like railway sleepers or logs stacked six or seven high and partly covered over the top with a snowy tarpaulin. It was strange though; the sun was reflecting and sparkling off what looked like little diamonds on the ends of each log. Seeing him staring over at the pile, one of the stretcher-bearers hanging onto the side of the truck said, "I wouldn't look too closely mate!" Chris thought: what's he on about? Why would he say that? Then the penny dropped. It wasn't railway sleepers or logs. The sun was shining off the studs in the soles of dead soldier's boots, lots of them!

Chapter 6

March 1917, Absolute Bliss!

Although in pain with his foot and it now looking as though it had been badly burnt, he had taken a bath, been given clean clothes, a bed with sheets, and was in a warm dry room, but best of all, it was quiet. There were cries and some noise from men in the wards and the rumbling like thunder of distant guns, but for the first time in months he could think. It was a very different world; it was just like experiencing time travel. Here people spoke softly to each other instead of shouting, the politeness of hearing people say, "Excuse me", "Thank you very much", "Would you like…?"

It seemed all rather odd to Chris that people could communicate without using expletives! He slept like never before, and oh to be clean, he hadn't realised that sweet, strange smell that had become the norm was him, rather than his surroundings. As soon as he could he wrote home to reassure David and Ellen he was alright, and they were so relived. His parents' previous letters had been returned to them unopened without explanation, so for a full two or three weeks they had feared the worst, each day hoping and praying the telegram boy or vicar would not be calling in.

In one of their letters, Chris read in disbelief as they told him of a German Zeppelin bombing raid over Derbyshire on 31st January. It had killed seven people at the Stanton Iron Works at Ilkeston, and there were also causalities when they had targeted Loughborough and Burton upon Trent. To Chris it seemed as if someone had pressed a fast forward button: the first manned flight had only taken place when he was born, now the skies above him today were full of planes, the bloody things, and what with Zeppelins bombing home! Everyday there was just so much to take in.

Looking around at the other chaps, Chris's injury was trivial, he could get around with his stick and sat for hours playing drafts or chequers with fellow patients, and being waited on by hand his recovery was slow but steady. Having his dressing changed every day and the frozen skin cut away it had stopped any infection and it was now scarring over nicely, but just like a burn the new skin was thin and delicate. Eventually he learnt to walk unaided by rolling his foot slightly and putting his weight on the outside, so apart from looking like a Charlie Chaplin tribute act he was OK. It was late April 1917 when he was discharged back up the line initially to be kept in reserve, but then was sent to help at the very field hospital that had saved his foot, partly as they had recognised he had learnt first-aid training and skills when he was in Northumberland, but also to help him recuperate fully.

As spring gave way to summer 1917, the offensives on all fronts were back in full flow. Chris was sent this time toward Ypres where the line had been pushed backwards and forwards, the British throwing massive resources there, realising it had to be held at all costs as it was such a significant gateway to the front. From what he had heard, Pete and Arthur had not made it through the earlier spring skirmishes, so he was teamed up with two new recruits straight from Belton MGC, they seemed so young and made him feel like a seasoned campaigner. It was a two-way association, they relished the vast experience he could offer and in return did more of the physical work of digging out etc. It was full on, the Germans relentless in pushing on every inch of the front line, so Chris, Frank and Sid were constantly used to give cover during attack and sent to hold and defend any hard-won ground.

The two weeks on at the front were sometimes stretched to three even nearly four before they were relieved to fall back to the support lines, where even then it was often fraught with danger. Nerves were running high, and the pressure from above to achieve these pencil-drawn lines on a map was huge.

In August 1917, Chris came across Charlie Chambers for the first time, as he was now under his leadership as a sectional commander. Charlie, a very dapper looking chap with airs and graces well above his station, was an ex-Boots the chemist warehouseman from Arnold in Nottingham and had signed up immediately as war broke out. He saw the whole thing as a great opportunity to better himself, and it was not through his natural ability as a leader, but by attrition that he had advanced up the ranks. He was a yes man, an army man knowing the King's rules inside out, as if he had written them himself. If he couldn't win men's hearts with leadership and respect, he would have no qualms in pushing them to the limit with chapter and verse. No one liked him, and they all tried to avoid his command if possible, even sometimes putting themselves in a more dangerous situation if led by a commander with whom they had greater respect.

The biggest fear of all men at this time was gas. The Germans had experimented early in the war and seen how devastating it was to the fighting troops, and its legacy physiologically was very powerful. As the stalemate continued, the Germans would try anything to break through. Late one day in September, Chris and his two apprentices were walking back from the front, across a field, which had some tree stumps along one side so men and materials were able to pass and keep close in for cover.

As they walked, a shell burst 200 yards or so over to their left. They carried on walking without too much concern, they just kept on walking; it was just a random shell, a normal daily occurrence. Then a second shell landed, but this time there was no explosion with the accompanied flying mud and debris, just a very loud 'plop'. Everyone knew instantly what this meant: the Germans had used the first shell as a target marker before firing a gas canister that had ruptured on landing, throwing its lethal liquefied chemical contents all around, which as it slowly mixed with air turned into a ground hugging, thick grey mist. There was panic from everyone, all shouting, "Gas, gas, gas, lads!"

It doesn't matter how many times this procedure is practised; when the time comes it is terrifying. Chris pulled on the canvas hood, biting down on the mouthpiece, and then trying to tuck it into his tunic and button it up as much as possible around his neck. His breathing was heavy and forced, he tried to calm himself down, and looking through the round windows of the hood he could see men running in all directions trying to get away from this unseen terror. Chris looked at what was left of the trees then the smoke to see if he could see which way the wind was blowing, which was at 45 degrees from behind him, so he worked out he was still in line of the flow. It looked and felt illogical, but he decided to run towards the shell so that he could get behind it and into clean air.

He started moving backwards, back towards the front. Running as best he could and sounding like a steam engine he passed men going the other way, trying to shout at them and gesticulate, they ignored him. More shells were coming in. Chris looked again at their smoke, he was sure he had made the right call, but now he realised he was putting himself in danger of the front line, he was exposed. Jumping into a trench or shell hole for protection was the worst thing he could do as this poisoned gas was heavier than air. It seemed to attack any delicate sensitive skin areas, the human lymph glands being very vulnerable to any contact, so exposed underarms and necks meant it would kill very quickly.

Most cases were disabling and extremely painful, but recoverable. It attacked the body's numerous soft skin folds, between fingers, underarms, behind the ears and knees, where this tender skin would react with the chemical causing severe blistering. Chris's hands and fingers felt funny and they started to itch. It's mustard gas, he thought. It blisters when it comes in contact with skin, so one breath and the lining of his lungs would become inflamed, drowning him in his own fluids.

He had managed to cross the field diagonally and could see some other men in a trench, this time without masks, shouting and waving for him to come over. He jumped down into this supply area and pulled off the canvas hood, gasping cold sweet air as sweat ran down his neck from his hair plastered to his head.

"Watcha mate!" said a soldier in a cockney accent, forcing a water bottle to his lips. God, that tasted so good! Chris then poured it over his head and the back of his hands, which seemed to take the sting away, and then as if by magic another guy appeared with army issue gas cream and a pack of butter and quickly rubbed that on too, which amazingly seemed to work. Other men poured tinned milk on the chemical burns, it probably had only marginal power but at least it was cold and sterile.

Others had joined them and were sat catching their breath. They looked backwards with field glasses and could see many had not made it. Some lay contorting on the ground; others were being led away, a hand on each other's shoulders, crocodile fashion. Where were Sid and Frank? They had been twenty yards behind so in theory should be safe. Chris thought the best thing was to stay put till the dawn Stand-To, report in what had happened, and then make his way back to the support trench, under the cover of darkness to catch up with his platoon there. It was a logical strategy, no point wandering about unprotected, he had left his gun and half his equipment as he ran for safety, so had to beg and borrow what bits he could from these Essex lads and try and settle down till night fall.

Christ! Chris awoke with a start. Reveille! It was 5.30am. The previous day's high dose of adrenalin and exhaustion must have caused him to sleep right through. He duly reported in with the officer in charge who verbally reprimanded him for not reporting in the day before, then made him do the hideous basic trench latrine duties until the following nightfall when he would be sent back to the support trench.

A near full moon with intermittent cloud, so the worst conditions for trying to creep out of the trench and back along the fallen tree line. As the clouds would randomly clear Chris would throw himself to the floor not wanting to stand out in this brilliant moonlight, then as the shadows appeared once more he would run as close to the ground as he could, stopping behind whatever shelter was there to catch his breath. This was a double-edged sword, with German marksmen at the rear and British trigger-happy guards looking in his direction for any sign of movement. With a near full moon they would be anticipating enemy action. Then there were the sappers roaming around, laying telephone lines and repairing barbed wire defences, each team would also have a look-out ready to fire at anything that moved.

Chris fell across such a team at work but managed to get the words "Forester, Sherwood Forester" out before they fired. They signalled back to the trench with a flashlight to say "Stray, returning home". Chris finally dropped down into the safety of the trench and made his way ever further back, stopping with a group of men who were sitting around a brazier. They plied him with hot sweet tea and the inevitable constant supply of Woodbines, before he took a quick catnap, and then it was time to report in at reveille.

Chris wasn't expecting a fanfare from anyone, but as he entered the semi-underground command post he had a feeling of self-satisfaction that he had made it through against all the odds and was able to stand there and report back for duty. So, to be faced with an instant barrage of verbal abuse from Charlie Chambers for his recent absenteeism was one thing, but to then be officially accused of being absent without leave, dereliction of duty and the abandonment of military equipment, was outrageous and totally unfair. No matter how much Chris protested his innocence and that he had reported into the Essex chaps who could verify his story, this was not even considered. These were very serious charges, the first two could carry the death penalty if proven, and Charlie was in his true element, being totally dogmatic and working to the letter of the rule book. Chris was charged and duly arrested and held in detention in a small outbuilding with two other guys, one who had got drunk on pilfered rum and another for fighting, both trivial offences compared to Chris's situation.

After two days of sleeping rough on the straw floor, at least it was dry, Chris was taken out and told to wash, shave and change into cleaner clothes, obviously second hand and with no insignia at all, but much better than he had been wearing for six weeks. He was taken to an outside table, where a senior officer was seated with Charlie Chambers to his right and another uniformed secretary of some sort. In official language the charges were read out and Charlie, true to form, degraded Chris in every way he could.

The only redeeming news was that the Essex lads had vouched for his encampment with them and that he had been present at reveille, so the first and most serious charge of desertion was not upheld. It was also only now that Chris learnt that the other two chaps in his team had perished.

Without further ado he was sentenced to Field Punishment Number One, which in the British army rule book required the said subject to be tied to a post or wheels of a field gun for a period of four hours at a time; a very shameful situation, so that fellow soldiers could clearly see what would happen to any soldier who was weak and had not followed orders to the letter. The other two reprobates were fined, dismissed and sent straight back to front line duties.

Once sentencing was passed, Chris was taken back to the outbuilding from where he would be sent forward in the morning for his punishment. He was woken early, just given time to wash and grab some bread and tea, before being marched unceremoniously forward to the gun battery position. Upon arrival, he was greeted by a smiling Charlie Chambers who re-read the charges and army regulations regarding his punishment.

As the field guns had been ensconced for such a long time their gun carriages had been withdrawn to help bring other materials forward, so, totally against army recommendations, Chris was tied in a crucifix position to one of the gun's large metal wheels. There were jeers and mud throwing from some who passed by and thought the opportunity was good sport, but overall everyone who passed just thought "poor bastard" and "there for the grace of God".

In this position the blood drains from outstretched arms and a mixture of cramp and pins and needles is the first agonising feeling, the knees go which in turn pulls on the wrist rope bands, so it becomes a cycle of pain relief replaced by pain increase. All the times at Mount Zion Church Chris had looked up at the stained-glass figure of Christ, his restraints a thousand times worse, but he now knew of the total anguish he must have suffered.

Just as he was halfway through his four-hour stint, he was pulled out of a dream-like state by the sound of a whistle and men running everywhere shouting orders "Prepare Battery". A gunnery sergeant came over pulling a knife from his pocket ready to cut Chris free, only to be stopped by Charlie's order: "Leave that man!"

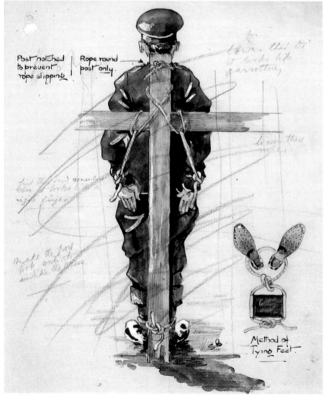

Field punishment No. 1

63

"But," retorted the gunner, but Charlie reprimanded him, threatening him with the same punishment if he went anywhere near Chris. Chris suddenly felt as though his insides had been stamped on by twenty horses, as the boom rushed through his body and out through his ears. The world was turned upside down, the straps to his ankles almost breaking his bones against the steel wheels. Chris's mind was racing: "Oh my God, they are firing the bloody gun!"

A second round was fired, and the same agony shot through his body. He felt his head smash into the steel spoke, then the stream of warm blood running down his neck. Seeing this, the lead gunner cut Chris's straps and let him fall in a lump onto the floor. That was the last Chris could remember. They left him there, while several more shots were fired off and then he was loaded onto a stretcher and taken back towards a medical facility, where they bandaged his head and bruised wrists and ankles and then let him sleep off the trauma.

A few days later, he was passed A1 and sent back to a reserve trench. Charlie realised he had crossed the line, though not from any empathy he may have had with Chris, so never continued with the full Field Punishment. He knew he had exceeded his authority in quite a blatant way that left him vulnerable to the same rule book he adhered to, so from then on, he distanced himself from Chris, no doubt finding another victim to focus on. He knew all Chris had to do was make an official complaint and it would be Charlie standing in front of his superiors.

In the meantime, Chris had time to think. He genuinely was the nicest man in the world, honest, thoughtful, someone who had empathy for everyone's ills, and a real pleasure for all to be with. But inside he was on fire with the anger he felt for the injustice and treatment he had suffered. The tribunal was one thing, which Chris could see was just an unfortunate interpretation of rules and discipline which were so important to hold all these people together against such odds. Even its implementation he could reconcile with, but it was the true sadistic nature of how this was staged via Charlie that made his blood boil.

Chris turned to his Bible for support and read passages of forgiveness, turning the other cheek, but he could not forgive that man, it was a constant dull pain that would not go away. He had never felt such hatred towards anyone in his life before; even towards the Hun he felt nothing. This was a war and he was fighting a just cause and doing his job as best he could for King and Country, and all the time merely wanting to survive and return home, but that Charlie, he was an out and out bastard. He was someone who saw war as a great opportunity to advance both socially and career wise, and in these violent times, an excuse to be able to express his genuine cruel streak. Chris thought if there wasn't a war, Charlie undoubtedly would have been one of those men who victimised and beat his wife and kids. He wasn't brave in any way, just a downright bully, revelling in his vindictive behaviour, which in this strange time and environment he could exploit and get away with.

Another five days in reserve, Chris was able to rest, eat properly, write home a chipper letter, and gather new issue clothing and equipment in readiness for redeployment to the forward trenches. Now formed back into yet another new machine gun crew, Chris was this time teamed up with Cyril, an old hand, and James aged 18, a fresh-faced lad from Mansfield who they took under their wing and familiarised him with the equipment, all the time giving him reassurances that he would be OK in their care if he listened to all the now vast experience these two men had to offer. I say 'men', but Chris was still only just 19 and Cyril 20.

Chapter 7

Spring 1918

The mundane ritual of trench life carried on as normal, the winter had been milder than 1917 and the days were now just starting to draw out, which meant both sides were preparing for the next big push. The British lines had been virtually static, which was good in that it was holding back the Germans, but everyone knew it was a stalemate and they had to go forward to win the war. They all noticed there was a significant difference in the equipment coming through, together with supplies of food and clothing, now that the USA had joined in. There were good and bad feelings towards them. Why had it taken them so long to come on board?

They were seen to be taking the glory, leaving the old guard still doing the daily dirty work, but then the stories of their first naive interventions came through of intolerable losses, they hadn't learnt anything from the earlier British struggle. The signs were there again of the preparation for something big, more regular bombardments from the British guns, more men and equipment flooding forward, and with the skies clear they were full of planes from both sides, each one trying to survey what was happening below. Chris and his mates would sit and watch them tumbling about up above, often firing off at them if an enemy plane swooped down to escape his rival. But it was common to see one of them catch fire and fold, somersaulting into the ground. "Poor buggers" the troops would say, "Wouldn't get me up there!" However, of the 16,000 deaths in this new air warfare, well over half were due to mechanical failures of one sort or another. So it was actually 'gravity' that killed far more of these trailblazing pilots, than their German opponents.

Our new 'Air Force', which is celebrating its centenary, on the 1st April 2018, did learn from these mechanical failings. The stringent safety checks and procedures which are now in place, to deliver consistent reliability, were all implemented after a shortcoming had been be seen to have caused a fatality, or endangered life.

April 6th was the day all this preparation had been leading up to. Chris and his fellow MCGs were shown a map of where the line was now and the target the front needed to reach to be a success. Half a mile! Didn't sound much but on the map every 100 yards was another trench, yet another obstacle which would cost hundreds of lives at best or thousands, if stubbornly defended. The night of the 5th at evening reveille the trenches were crammed with troops. The battery was still ongoing from the British guns, with the sight and sound of hundreds of glowing shells whooshing overhead, and then the flash and five seconds later the rumble just like a thunderstorm, so no one could sleep. Chris was sent ahead again to the right where he and several other MGC teams were dug in and preparing to open up the battle after the artillery had finished and then defend any repulse action from the Hun.

After hours of shelling, at 6am on the button, the whistles could be heard and the MGC opened up, spraying the forward trenches to try and stop the Hun emerging from underground safety and setting up their own gun positions. On the next whistle they were to watch for the infantry coming out over the top and support them as they headed to the German position. The machine gunners were then to split, half defensive, while the rest move forward to establish a new nest and make safe for the next wave of infantry to move forward again. As Chris had a final sweep of the enemy lines before his team moving forward, he could see the men piling out over the top, marshalled on by an officer blowing a whistle and waving a hand gun. It was him, Charlie!

It was in an instant, Chris's hand pulled to the right too much on his final sweep and he saw Charlie spin awkwardly and fall backwards. "Come on Chris we have to go!" was the shout from the rest of his crew as they started to dismantle the gun and move forward. It was totally surreal. Had what he thought just happened really happened? There was no time to think, so throwing the heavy hot barrel onto his well-padded shoulder, he followed the others in his team through muddy craters and jumped down into a German trench.

It was a forward supply trench that was zig-zagging backwards, so the idea was to get as far as they could, other Forester lads were throwing grenades ahead to clear the trench so they could set the nest up again. Suddenly there was a brilliant white light and a gush of heat from a shell bursting in the air over to Chris's left! (The nearest any of us will possibly come to experience this feeling, is stepping out of a cold, dark air-conditioned plane and taking that first step onto the tarmac of a hot holiday destination, as the bright light dazzles you and the warm air envelopes you.) In the same millisecond a large piece of shrapnel smashed into the barrel of the gun with such force it fractured the water jacket and tossed it out of his grip.

Without the protection of the barrel he now would lay incapacitated. His left forearm was peppered with light shot; more 10p sized pieces dented his helmet and ricocheted off, just as an L-shaped piece tore into his gunner's waistcoat, slicing the canvas ribbing, but it held and was still sufficiently robust to stop it penetrating his torso. It did however continue downwards, being rebuffed by the triangle of leather at the rear of his braces, then it tore into the soft muscle and flesh as it exited his trousers and slammed into the earth, where it sizzled in the wet clay. Then a strange, floating feeling took hold of Chris as the full force of the shockwave threw him through the air, just like Superman, with his left arm straight out and his right arm back and below him. Chris saw the earth coming towards him in slow motion, knowing it was going to hurt, and he landed face down in the mud.

No breath! Why can't I breathe? Then the gasp of air as the wind knocked out of him suddenly refilled his lungs to bursting. "What the f…?" Chris's mind tried to make sense of what had happened. With his quick very shallow breaths, he started to access how he was, felt his left hand, OK. He wriggled and stuck his toes into the mud to lift the weight off his right arm which he brought up to wipe the clay from his mouth. There was a little blood and he felt the tingling of a fat lip coming but he was OK.

Slowly at first, but gradually growing in momentum, a dull ache appeared in Chris's lower back. Aaargh! My hip! I must have landed on my back, thought Chris, as he moved his arm back to rub his pain better, only then slowly realising that the wetness he felt against his body wasn't clay or water; it was warm, very warm. He pulled his hand back and saw it was covered in soil and blood. A panic set in: I am bleeding, bleeding a lot, this isn't a scratch this is serious. He lay there trying to move more into the recovery position, and shouted for help, but then it dawned on him how quiet it was, he didn't even hear his own voice only the vibrations inside. There was a strange high-pitched buzzing in his ears but only distant muffled sounds of shouting and gun fire. The blast had temporarily made him totally deaf. His hearing recovered, but I can always remember his large pink NHS hearing aids. He shouted again, "Help! Help!" but nothing. He felt his hands go cold, he was shivering, his throat was so dry…and then he blacked out.

Coming to later, he was face down on a muddy stretcher, bouncing over rough ground, being carried by two men who flicked mud up into his face as they struggled to carry him along a service trench without slipping themselves. He was pushed frequently to one side as other men moved forward past them, each jolt agony. Chris threw up; a mixture of rock and roll, fear and the unbelievable pain in his back. He felt the urgent need to go to the lavatory, but any attempt at muscle control in that area was sheer agony, so suddenly there was another warm feeling in his blood-soaked trousers.

He must have passed out again and came around this time still lying face down on his stretcher, but as he looked to his left he was in a long line of fellow patients outside a large canvas marquee with a red cross. A pretty young nurse gave him a drink from a water bottle and lit him a cigarette, lifted the dressing on his back to assess his injury, allowing in cold air and immediately the dull pain ragged again. He was given a large shot of morphine, and instantly drifted into oblivion, having the most surreal dreams, now covered with a blanket, onto which they had pinned a piece of paper with the large letter C. This was the army's first attempt at triage, so soldiers could receive the appropriate treatment, the most serious taking priority A.

As Chris drifted in and out of his morphine induced sleep, the next time he came round he was in a camp bed in a large tent, again face down, and he could feel tight bandages around his middle and see a frame over his back to keep the weight of blankets from him.

"Er ya go pal."

It was the best cup of tea he had ever had, served hot in an enamel mug resting on the floor with a rubber tube as a straw and what tasted like six sugars. Later, when the male nurse from Bolton came back with a biscuit and bread (his first meal in 36 hours), Chris asked what had happened. "You've been hit with shrapnel in the arse mate," he said coldly. "It's your ticket home, and you'll still be a pretty boy, as long as you don't drop your keks. It must have been a grenade or shell. Lucky they pulled you out when they did. You've lost a lot of blood."

Chris lay there trying to pull together all he could remember, not a lot at first but over the next few days the pain subsided and his mind was set free to roam. He started to remember things in reverse order. First the flash of the explosion throwing him in the air, the jumping down into the trench, running over the shell craters carrying the barrel, then the vision flashed through his mind of a twirling Charlie falling backwards into the trench. He felt sick, and clammy. It was his worst nightmare slowly becoming a reality.

He put it to the back of his mind, he must be hallucinating. But over the next few weeks the vision kept coming back stronger and in more detail. He would wake in the middle of the night sobbing at what he had done, but along with all the other residents who cried out and had bad dreams, his tears were taken as normal. With more rest he was moved further and further back towards the coast, he too was now heading back to the military hospital in Leicester on the very same train he had glimpsed over a year earlier. He would now be one of those starry-eyed men laid on a stretcher across seats who had looked through him and the lads as they had travelled south.

It was May, and David and Ellen were there as soon as they heard Chris was back in the UK. Travelling down early from Chesterfield on a day return they brought clothes, fruit and letters of best wishes from all in Chesterfield. There was, to his surprise, even a card from a certain young lady called Frances who had heard he was injured, via Mr Treece's communal bakery. Having lost her intended at Arras eight months earlier she had empathy with Chris's parents, and remembered Chris as 'that nice, chatty young man'.

The damage to Chris's back was slow to heal; the dressing to his lower back having to be packed and changed frequently as infection was the main concern. The blast had ripped flesh and peeled away some muscle, so it must have hit him sideways on. He was lucky, no random shrapnel impelled deep inside, contaminated with pieces of dirty clothing, so it was recoverable. His back muscles, however, weakened for the rest of his life, were aided by a support corset that, as a child I remember, always seemed to be on the washing line or clothes horse by the fire so no one would know. So many others returning home wore prominent ghastly reminders of what they went through.

He was back at home for the summer so was able to build up his

71

strength with short walks with David. This time no long walking adventures over Linacre and beyond, but he found swimming helped enormously with his movement, so he joined the Inkerman Swimming Club. Based in a large clay quarry where Rockingham Close Ashgate is now, it had changing rooms and a tea hut, diving boards, and apparently an unlimited depth.

He became such a strong swimmer that for many years later he was part of the Boxing Day 'break the ice clan', including Freddie Vickers who he would work with at Brampton Gas. Freddie later taught me and Brian to swim at Markham Baths on Chatsworth Road. Chris had to report into the St James Hall, and was accessed as to his capabilities and physical fitness; he was now deemed unfit for full active duty and wasn't going to be sent back to front line.

However, the army, not wanting to waste any resource, were arranging to send him back to Grantham to train other recruits at the Belton Camp. This had grown to twice the size; it even had its own rail station now and supported the newer heavy brigades of motorcycle with side-car gunners (totally inappropriate in the soft clay and trenches) and tank corps. This new weapon was the only way the stalemate of trench warfare could be broken. These early tanks were agricultural at best, the large ones had the engine exposed in the middle of the vehicle so the troops were more likely to die from carbon monoxide poisoning than a shell.

They also trained Chris as a first-aider and stretcher-bearer, when he could walk with a stretcher, but getting someone off the ground with his straight corseted back was near impossible. It was whilst he was being assessed at St James Hall one day that he saw a list of Sherwood Foresters men who had been killed, and as if his eyes were pulled by a strange force, the name Charlie Chambers jumped out from all the other names. Chris had managed to put his nightmare to the back of his mind and pretend it had not happened, but this brought it back with a vengeance, it was there in black and white. He had killed that man!

The tens of others did not play on his conscience; they were the nameless, faceless enemy. But this man, Charlie Chambers…. He could see him with his yellow teeth, smell his tobacco breath, and picture the glare of those angry eyes. A raw feeling welled up inside Chris and the next minute he broke down sobbing uncontrollably.

He could not go back and put it right; he could not even tell someone to share the load. It was locked deep inside and weighed heavy on his mind and in his subconscious, there was no escape. This feeling was constant and was not going away. Even in church on Sunday, he could only sit staring at the crucifixion above, feel the tight straps again on his wrists and ankles. How could Jesus look so calm and serene and show forgiveness to his tormentors? Chris still felt such hate, but at the same time felt deep remorse for what he had done. He had taken someone's life in pure anger. For Chris this was the ultimate sin; how could he possibly redeem himself? The only way to keep his sanity and find this inner redemption was to help save others, to save lives that would otherwise be lost, to recalibrate the balance of life he had taken.

Chapter 8

Belton Park, 1918

Chris enjoyed his new life back at Belton Park, his experience and skill being put to great use with these new recruits. His strength continued to improve. He certainly wasn't as nimble as he used to be, but apart from that wretched corset, he was doing OK.

At the beginning of March 1918, the Kaiser was throwing everything he had at the Allied lines. At certain points on the front, the Allies were outnumbered by the German forces, six to one. German aircraft would often fly over dropping leaflets saying, "Hey Tommy, what are you dying for? The Americans won't be over here for another year."

It was also early 1918 that the Germans introduced the name 'stormtrooper' for the first time. These elite forces were armed with a new, much lighter, Krugergrenade, enabling the soldier to carry more of them. They were also designed to explode within a small area, unlike the heavy British No. 5 Mills bombs, designed to be thrown over a defensive wall, which would probably do as much harm to the British Tommy as he advanced as to his opponents. These stormtroopers advanced so rapidly, covering each other as they did so, that they took the Allied lines by total surprise. With this new tactic the Germans advanced across a 50-mile front, three miles deep into Allied held territory. It came at a cost of 38,000 Allied troops, but also 40,000 German.

At the Battle of Chemins De Mans, the Germans were now outnumbering the Allies by 4:1, they advanced 12 miles in one day and were now only 39 miles from Paris. Their huge guns were firing 264 lb shells 24 miles into space, falling back to earth 75 miles away. They killed over 250 Parisians and destroyed many buildings. It was now looking as though Paris could fall. But in June 1918, US General John Pershing came over with one million men and their might was instantly seen at the Battle of Belleau Wood, with their first full-on engagement. Not learning from the early years of the war, they lost over 1,000 men on the very first day, but their supply chain of men and equipment was overpowering and the advance on Paris was finally halted.

The French also learnt from the US about mass production: at the start of 1914 they only had 170 motor trucks, whereas now they could support their troops with 37,000 vehicles. The Germans had 749 big guns, but with the support of the US there were now 2,000 Allied ones. The Germans had 100 planes, against an unbelievable 1,900. The Allies had developed the tank corps to a strength of 100, the Germans nil, though they were evenly matched with the number of divisions, at ten each. The Allied/US divisions numbered 15,000 men in each, the Germans 6,500. So the sheer number of troops and machinery now totally outnumbered the Germans, and with the input of the USA there was an inevitable conclusion.

As the Kaiser said on the 8th August 1918, it was the "blackest day" for Germany. In just four days 40,000 men were taken prisoner. Morale was very fragile and the German troops who once fought to the death were now half starved and ill-equipped and would quite happily surrender. They all knew the end was coming and just wished their commanders would see sense and capitulate, instead they still threw men's lives away like paper.

The Allies had finally got mastery of all the armed forces with their full blockades at sea, won at great expense at the Battle of Jutland, and it was now completely sapping Germany of its food imports and manufacturing materials. The Allies had massive air superiority, and their armies had the manpower and endless equipment, especially new heavy guns. They were able to master the skies and take detailed photos of the enemy lines, creating precise maps to accurately fire upon held positions, without having to commit and lose men. Under this intense pressure, and with the German soldiers knowing that not only they but their loved ones at home were starving because of the blockades, morale crumbled.

The US 46th North Midland Division crossed the canals in borrowed channel ferry lifeboats, to storm the Hindenburg Line, the final holding position of the once mighty German army. They managed to break through and create a bridgehead, and once the weakness was seen, on 30th September, 1.2 million men were committed and a 40-mile stretch was taken with ease. I say 'with ease', only 83 men were killed per mile taken, as opposed to the 8,000 casualties per mile at Passchendaele in 1915. The Kaiser begged the US and Britain for an amnesty, and for the

German Royal family to be able to stay in power, but to no avail, and he was forced to abdicate on the 9th November.

The armistice was agreed for the 11th November at 11am. Even then, 12,000 men from both sides were killed and injured in these final few days of conflict. The very last man known to have been killed was an American called Henry Gunter, who, ironically, was from a from a second-generation German immigrant family. For two years he had lived in and endured all the horrors of trench warfare, only for it to end so poignantly. He was killed at one minute to eleven by a German soldier, emptying his machine gun prior to that final whistle at 11am on the 11th.

The Allies were ill-prepared for this victory, and the wave of ill feeling by the common men who had been used as pawns in this war of Empires was palpable. One third of the men in Europe were now dead, and the remainder wanted changes and a new beginning. Chris, thinking his war was now over and he could go home and start his own life, was informed that everyone from the Belton MGC was to be sent overseas back to France, Belgium and Germany. There was a massive power vacuum until the official signing of the Treaty of Versailles and the easiest way to control people was with a strategically installed machine gun. One machine gun nest could control the same number of population as it would take thousands of troops to manage.

For Chris to go back over to France against the rejoicing homecoming tide was tough, physically and emotionally, this was where he faced his nemesis of Life and Faith. The thing that shocked Chris most was how quickly things had changed: streets had been cleaned and shell-shot buildings were all being repaired. Snow would fall, and as it lay heavy, it made everything look clean and virginal, when in reality underneath the earth was scarred and deformed.

Life had quickly turned back to being relatively normal; it was as though that entire painful nightmarish world he had lived through had never existed. Thousands of people were now constantly on the move and they were the things not able to be repaired so quickly. Many were still so traumatised with that cold, empty eyed expression, still so tense and expecting…something that wasn't there any more. Daily life now was so mundane that they couldn't take it in, and they seemed to be frightened of believing they could be happy again.

Five years earlier the world had all been so upbeat and positive with everyone having a real zest for life, but now there was an emotional vacuum; even that dark humour had evaporated as the perpetual adrenalin rush left a stark, numb reality of "what was that all about?"

So, the riots and revolts Chris's MGC was sent over to control never happened, people had no fight left in them, they all just wanted to go home. There was some widespread pilfering and Chris's MGC was stationed to protect a series of huge French grain stores and adjacent flour mills. But Chris and his fellow soldiers found themselves spending more time aiding the Red Cross and other humanitarian organisations than being involved in any military action for the British army.

Chapter 9

December 13th 1918, Influenza

At least Chris was well billeted: clean, warm and dry this time, well-fed and in good health. This was so crucial for the next life trial to hit him. As shown on his medical card on the December 13th 1918, he was struck down with influenza. Known as 'Spanish Flu', it actually came over from America in June 1918 and had steadily taken its toll. Over one million men had been hospitalised, of which 45,000 were to die before November, and it was suggested millions more died as they all dispersed home around the world.

Chris was so weak he could not stand up and was taken on a stretcher to the medical station. All the orderlies and doctors looked like something from 'the great plague', dressed in white smocks and wearing face masks, rubber gloves and wellies. They listened to his gurgling chest, red raw from infection, and his shallow breathing.

They passed him straight over to a canvas ward where similarly dressed staff made him comfortable and made him breathe hot, steamy

Field hospital for 'flu victims

First Name:	C
Surname:	Loveridge
Index Number of Admission:	6576
Rank:	Private
Service Number:	30695
Ailment:	Influenza
Date of Admission for Original Ailment:	13/12/1918
Date Transferred to Sick Convoy:	15/12/1918
Date of Transfer From Sick Convoy:	Direct Admission
Notes written in the Observations Column:	No. 22 Ambulance Train.
Religion:	Wesleyan
Regiment:	Machine Gun Corps
Battalion:	3rd Company (Why is this important?)
Other unit info:	3rd Division

Chris' medical admission record

vapours from a distinctive Brampton pottery earthenware jug, with a towel over his head. Whatever was in it was enough to blow your head off, but it did ease the tight chest pain and allowed him to sleep and keep his strength. Once his condition had stabilised, on the 15th December, he was transferred out.

This flu was so virulent; it was known to take people overnight. One group of ladies who played bridge one evening with no sign of infection woke in the morning with two succumbed, both had died by lunchtime. It was just luck and a strong constitution that separated the winners and losers. Usually flu attacks the very young who have no immune defence and the old as they are weak. This flu was different: it hit the 20-40-year age groups the hardest. While the youngest immune system saw it as new and fought back with antibodies, and the old seemed to already have the antibodies, the 20-40 age groups just succumbed in their thousands. This was also the age of the solider who had fought, so to come through all that and to be taken from your loved ones by flu was cruel, to say the least.

Chris, who was just over 20, was one of the lucky ones. Sent back home again, he was still weak and very chesty, and was finally medically discharged from the army with bronchitis at the end of January 1919. His war was over and he looked forward with relief to getting on with his own life. Back home with David and Ellen at Chester Street, he relished all the simple mundane things of normal life he had dreamt of when he was 'over there', but his youthful 'get up and go' had evaporated and he seemed and acted a lot older than his age. Young boys like Chris at 17, and there were lots more as young as 15–16, had experienced more in four years than any generation before them. Not only through the trauma they had been witness to, they had also seen the rapid advance in technology and total change in society. Life had changed them all in the last four years and it had altered them irrevocably. All suffered from various forms of anxiety, ranging from survival guilt, physical trauma and what now would be called 'Post-Traumatic Stress Disorder' (PTSD).

All these mental scars and guilt issues had virtually no support or recognition from the British army or government institutions. Extreme 'shell shock' syndrome was identified, and treatment offered, but for most of these traumatised returning men, they only survived with the support and help of family and loved ones. As a consequence, however, over the years many a relationship fell apart from the sheer strain and incomprehension of what these guys had been through, there was no going back to a 'happy place' for many. Only the strong-minded or the ones who could lock it away were able to cope, even then it was only just below the surface of normal life.

But it wasn't quite a land fit for heroes, times were strange, society and life for all those at home had altered so much in such a short time, too. The old feudal society was no more, it had been a levelling of all men, and even the old wealthy families were now on hard times and struggling to adapt to this new world order. Their estates fell into ruin as the huge manpower previously used to support them was no longer there. Often the landed gentry had lost their heirs to these vast estates, so there was literally no one to take charge and run these complex agricultural and social systems. The government was bankrupt, meaning that taxes, death duties and rates were raised to try and refill the coffers, making so many of these old houses and estates a millstone for those left to inherit them. Often, the only way forward was to have them broken up and sold on, and even have them dismantled.

The *nouveau riche* of America eagerly imported chandeliers, fireplaces, carved oak panelling and stone features to decadently show off their new wealth. The prime example locally is Scarsdale Hall, which now stands as a skeletal shell, seen as you drive between junctions 29–30 on the M1, on the opposite hill to Bolsover Castle. Everything that could have been taken and resold was stripped away, and the farmland sold off.

Other ordinary men returning home found their jobs were now taken by women. After four years' experience of precision engineering, many factory owners found these women to be very highly skilled, and they could employ three highly skilled ladies for the price of two male labourers, so there was reluctance to let them go. Also, those women who weren't highly skilled and did the mundane repetitive work were happy to work for half the male pay, as long as they were in a female social group, something which would be frowned upon in our modern society.

Demand for many manufactured goods slowed, and jobs for these returning heroes were few and far between. With total state control of industry during the war, the glorious British Empire power plant had lost its impetuous. For example, the Scottish ship building industry fell from employing over 100,000 workers to 10,000. Many families were forced to decide that their only option was to emigrate to the new booming colonies of Canada and Australia, all looking for a better life.

Chris, like many more returning soldiers, eked out his severance pay as long as he could whist looking for work. He initially found work as a labourer at the coke ovens, ironically back up at Grassmoor. It was a very labour-intensive operation and physically challenging, especially for Chris with his weak back. However, he told us there was not always transport available so more than often he ended up walking there and back. This was on top of his ten-hour shift.

Later, in 1919, heavy industry had slowed so much as demand for coke for industrial furnaces fell dramatically. Chris and many other men were put on short time, so he had no choice but to look around for something else. Eventually through contacts with his brother, who was a gas lamplighter, he heard of a vacancy and was taken on with the Brampton Gas Works at West Bars. The town gas infrastructure

82

had been neglected and new gas feeds were needed, spreading their tentacles out to industry and housing developments around Chester-field. His weak back was sometimes limiting but he learnt threading and connecting the iron pipe work and became an invaluable part of the team.

He had re-ignited his friendship with Frances Boston who now worked at Shentall's grocers on Chatsworth Road near Bank Street. She worked with Chris's sister, Alice. As the shop stayed open till 8pm on Fridays and Saturdays, and Frances lived further up Old Hall Road on Brocklehurst Piece (opposite the Britannia Pub), Alice would often invite her back home for tea, and with Chris back home their relation-ship blossomed. After three years of courtship they were eventually married at St Thomas' Church, Brampton on the 29th January 1923.

Frances and Chris

They moved in with Frances's parents, Annie Boston (her father John Boston had died in 1914 of quinsy of the throat), her step-father Cecil Taylor and her brother Jack Boston, all at 9 Brocklehurst Piece. With all five living there in the small two-up-two-down, they had Joan in 1924 and Clifford in 1927 before moving to Charles Street to be in their first family home.

Christopher had survived against such unbelievable odds, starting with his childhood stroke, all that the MGC threw at him, plus his gassing, frostbite, field punishment, shrapnel wounds, flu, the Blitz in London and his 30 Park Drive-a-day habit, so all I can say is, "Thank you Granddad!" Thank you for passing on the amazing gift of life to

Ioan and Clifford

my mother, myself and Brian, our wonderful children and now amazing grandchildren. For all his positive service in the war, all the lives he saved with Red Cross, and particularly with his constant blood transfusions, and then all the people he rescued in the Blitz. He really did make such a positive difference to so many people's lives, and we all owe him such a debt of gratitude, but was it enough for him to equate to the one life he took that still haunted him?

We always visited on Saturday afternoons, and the long walk was always made bearable by the thought of sitting next to him while he watched the Saturday sport on TV. He would shout encouragement at the horse racing and he loved to watch the wrestlers throw each other out of the ring. We would play board games, especially drafts – no one could ever manage to beat him – and on a good day my two cousins Stephen and Andrew would be there too. I can still see him now semi

Chris in his car at Brocklehurst Piece

whistling, Woodbine in the corner of his mouth, blue bib and brace overhauls, white collarless shirt with rolled sleeves as he pushed me in his wheelbarrow back from the allotment at Goldwell Hill. The wheels squeaking and his studded boots clumping along the road as we returned to 18 Alexander Road West for a cup of tea with my Grandma Frances, my mum Joan and "our Brian" who had stayed to play Meccano. It was the same boots-off ritual and hand washing in the sink with red rubber nozzles, and then the room full of smoke and chatter.

This was the 60's, a time when everyone smoked, even my grandmother, who was a strict Methodist and awfully prim, would ask for "one of those mental cigarettes", her pronunciation was something that always amused my brother and me. So the fact that I would sit, making my grandfather's roll-up cigarettes with his fascinating rolling machine was never looked on as odd. It was while he was using his paraffin smelling lighter to offer a light to other people in the room, that I can remember I heard him mention the war for the first time. I could never understand why, as he sparked up his magical, smelly paraffin lighter, he would only light for two people at a time, then rest and spark it back to life again to offer a light to the next person. I can remember asking why he did this and being told, "It's unlucky".

He then told me of the story about the time when he fought in the trenches. As you lit your cigarette, the German snipers would be attracted to the light, and when you passed it to the next man they would take aim, so by the time it was given to the third person, well, his chances of enjoying a quiet smoke were pretty slim. This story has stayed with me ever since, and at a time when boys played cowboys and Indians or war games it was always a good tale to tell your mates.

This being one of many stories he would recall. He was very special, my grandfather, a lovely man, we had a special bond as I was named after him. However, I did have regrets when I started my first school as I could never spell Christopher, much to his amusement. As I write this I cannot imagine the memories he had running through his head daily, how he appeared so normal. But I can understand why he wanted to be so nice. He saw his four grandchildren as a new beginning, lives unspoilt, unblemished by the two wars that had had such an enormous effect on him.

Also amazing were all the great changes and things he saw for the first time: planes, cars, telephones, TV, space flight. But then there was still all the negative thoughts and memories he carried with him, that guilt would always be there. No wonder he was never happier than when he was on his allotment, alone with his thoughts and in his own controlled world of simplicity, beauty and more importantly, a life cycle he could nurture.

Before my eleventh birthday, I was with my mate Bryan Hall and his brother Jeremy. I was hanging upside down on the five-bar gate at the entrance to the three-corner field, half way along Ashgate Avenue, when I saw my upside-down mum walking purposefully up from our house at 85 Manor Road. Thinking I was in trouble again, I jumped down and came to meet her as I didn't want to be embarrassed in front of my mates by whatever I had done. Then I saw the look in her eyes and I knew what it was, it was the same wide terrified eyes that I saw three years earlier when my own father had died.

Thursday 30th September, a heart attack totally out of the blue, my perfect childhood world had disintegrated. Teenage boys need a man to look up to, listen to, and to model themselves on. I had transferred all that male love and bonding to my grandfather and now it was going to be taken from me a second time. Mum tried to be positive and remain calm, but she faltered and told me uncontrollably that we needed to get washed and catch the bus across town over to see Granddad, as soon as possible as he was asking for his grandchildren.

As we entered the downstairs hall of the flat at 11 Brindley Way, we were immediately hit by the same familiar thick odour, hard to describe, a sort of very sweet, boiled cabbage, partially disguised by Dettol and Jeyes Fluid. Having suffered a mild stroke and now having to stay in bed, controlling pressure bed sores with his wounds became an issue. Hence, this strange odour had been emanating from his lower back, his war wound finally taking hold of the tissues and turning to gangrene, his body now racked with sepsis, he was slowly drifting away.

We were marshalled into the bedroom to hold his hand and kiss him for the final time; I can remember running out to find Lego or anything to play with, anything to distract me from this pain that was rushing towards me again. It was those last few hours that I wasn't privy to, Mum told me he tightly held his 18th birthday Bible which he had taken to Flanders, repeating the Lord's Prayer, and asking if Joan thought he would get into heaven, because of "what I had done".

"What do you mean?" Mum asked.

"Because I got the bugger," he said.

"What do you mean, Dad?"

"That bastard that tied me to the wheel of the gun, I got him you know."

So there it was. My grandfather's deathbed confession. Stark, honest, heart-wrenching. As a machine gunner he had obviously killed tens, or even hundreds of men. Yet this did not affect his conscience so severely: they were the nameless, faceless dead of the other side. Yet the terrible, terrible guilt he felt for taking a single man's life in anger consumed him. I can still feel it as I write the words, heavy on this page.

Why did it matter so much to him? His strong religious upbringing was engrained deep inside. It was one thing to put them aside for the just cause and calling of King and Country, but Charlie's death was taken in anger, when he should have turned the other cheek as his gospel had instructed.

Joan looked for reassurance at my Grandma Frances, but her eyes told Joan that she had known a long time, Chris bearing his soul before they married, her redemption and support was pivotal. It now all fell into place. It explained the cries in the middle of the night. So that was the dark secret that Frances and Chris had skirted around as Joan and Clifford grew up asking what was wrong. They had been told about him being a marksman, they knew he had been tied to a gun, they listen to him talk of tripping up on other people's innards, the intense cold, the frostbite, the gas and shrapnel, and they lived through all his Blitz stories, but this was an even heavier burden to take on.

So that was it! That's why he tried to be so good, so perfect; to help others wherever and whenever he could. Still clasping his Bible that had been given to him by my Great- Grandfather David all those years ago, he seemed to finally find peace as he slipped away on the 11th April 1967.

With all the easy access to military records and family history I used that same Bible to research his war years. Working with my mum Joan and the old suitcase of photos etc., we managed to put together his story. When I had finished his brief military history I was chatting with Mum to try and fill in his family history, when she broke down and told me of his deathbed secret. I was not expecting that, but it explained an awful lot about the man I knew.

His story had to be told, I don't think it is a unique story, as in all that turmoil of destruction I bet all sorts of private retributions were enacted. But what about that other poor person, he also had the same right to return home, and get on with his life. Who he was I will never be able to find out. (I called him Charlie.) His name will undoubtedly be listed on a memorial somewhere, which his family would dutifully visit over the years, touch his name and honour him as being killed by those evil Germans, when in fact he was murdered by my own wonderful grandfather. Is what my grandfather did so wrong? Should he be considered a war criminal?

Why should the killing of hundreds of men whom you have never met or had any grievance with other than being in the wrong trench, be any different from killing someone who was much closer to you, but posed a greater threat to your very existence? God's testimony tells us that all life is sacred, so how can one be socially acceptable and the other so wrong? Can any of us honestly say that in that environment and in those circumstances we would have acted differently?

War is the battle for life: it triggers our primeval instincts to survive at any costs. "The Battle of Faith", well that comes later, much later when you are safe and warm and have time to contemplate and think about your actions. When I set off on this journey of discovery I did not expect to uncover even half of Christopher's incredible story.

I find it very poignant, how little did his father, my Great-Grandfather David Loveridge, know when he scribbled in that small Bible one hundred years ago, not only the enormity of the task he set in those written words, but what the true meaning of "The Battle of Life and Faith" would be!

Thank you so much
David
for all you do, Thank you for writing about my Dad. and always give me advice when J ask.
love you
Mum
xxx

Many thanks to Jenny Windle, my English teacher at Newbold Green School, who, when others thought I was a lost cause due to my dyslexia, encouraged me greatly.

Photographs, Illustrations and Acknowledgements:

1. Granddad in uniform, courtesy of Doubledutch
2. Granddad in suit, courtesy of Doubledutch
3. Granddad in St John uniform, courtesy of Doubledutch
4. Granddad on Parade, courtesy of Doubledutch
5. Granddad's Gas Works retirement, courtesy of Doubledutch
6. Joan in uniform WW2, courtesy of Doubledutch
7. Bible with barbed wire/bullet, courtesy of Doubledutch.
8. 86 Chester Street, courtesy of Doubledutch
9. Rear of 18 Alexander Road West and Lidl, courtesy of Doubledutch
10. Chain halyards, old gas works, courtesy of Doubledutch.
11. Enlisting poster, courtesy of Imperial War Museum
12. Recruitment at St James Hall, courtesy of Imperial War Museum
13. Enlistment details x 4, courtesy of Doubledutch
14. Vickers Machine Gun and Equipment, courtesy of Imperial War Museum
15. MGC transfer, courtesy of Doubledutch
16. MGC badge, courtesy of Imperial War Museum
17. Hooded MGC in action, courtesy of Imperial War Museum
18. MGC at Belton Park, courtesy of Imperial War Museum
19. Chris in forward trench, courtesy of Doubledutch
20. Frostbite, courtesy of Imperial War Museum
21. Wounded trolley, courtesy of NTM
22. Hospital carriage, courtesy of NTM
23. St John and Lancashire & Yorkshire Railway award, courtesy of NTM
24. Field Punishment Number 1 Post, courtesy of Imperial War Museum
25. Hospital transfer details, courtesy of Doubledutch
26. Flu Field Hospital, courtesy of Imperial War Museum
27. Wedding photo, courtesy of Doubledutch
28. Wedding photo, courtesy of Doubledutch
29. Chris in car Brocklehurst Piece, courtesy of Doubledutch
30. Validation from Joan, courtesy of Doubledutch